The Stinking Overthinking Trap

Break Free to Find Your Balance, Vitality, and Inner Calm

Barbara Heavens

Table of Contents

Introduction

We've all been there—tossing around at 2 a.m. with our brains on full blast, mentally rehearsing that awkward conversation with our boss for the 47th time. Or standing in the shower, replaying that stupid thing we said at a party *three years ago*. (Just me? No? Phew.) I call this the "stinking overthinking trap," when your mind gets caught in an endless game of mental pinball and the flippers just. won't. stop.

My personal overthinking low point? Probably that time, I spent two weeks agonizing over whether I should text "Thanks!" or "Thank you!" to my neighbor who watered my sad-looking houseplants while I was away. *Two weeks*, people. I even made a pros and cons list. (For the record, I went with "Thanks so much!"—the coward's compromise.)

Overthinking used to run my life. My brain was like that friend who texts you at midnight with "You up?" and then proceeds to analyze every interaction they had that day. Except it was *my own brain* doing this *to me*. The mental gymnastics were exhausting—I'd second-guess every decision, from "Should I change careers?" down to "Is this the right brand of toilet paper?"

The impact was real. Sleep? Ha! Good luck with that when your mind is staging Olympic-level worry competitions at 3 a.m. Focus? About as effective as trying to read a book while someone blasts an air horn in your ear. And don't get me started on my poor husband, who once had to sit through my 45-minute analysis of whether our waitress was subtly insulting my drink order. (Spoiler: She wasn't. She literally did not care about my mojito.)

If you're sitting there nodding so hard you're risking whiplash, you're not alone. We're living in the golden age of overthinking. Our phones ping with new things to worry about every 2.7 seconds. The news cycle makes sure we're constantly updated on fresh disasters to obsess over. And social media is basically an all-you-can-eat buffet for comparison anxiety.

I finally hit my breaking point after a particularly spectacular overthinking spiral about—I kid you not—whether my email sign-off sounded "too aggressive." (It was "Best regards." The horror!) I realized I was spending more time in my head analyzing life than actually, you know, *living* it.

So, I made changes. Not overnight, and definitely not perfectly. There were setbacks like that time I tried meditation and spent the entire 20 minutes mentally redecorating my living room and planning my grocery list. But gradually, I found what worked. The mental noise quieted down. I started sleeping better. I could watch a movie without pausing it six times to worry about whether I'd left the garage door open.

This book isn't some magical cure-all written by a perfectly enlightened guru who has transcended all human worries. Hell no. I still overthink sometimes! Just last week, I spent an hour wondering if my neighbor thinks I'm weird because I awkwardly waved at her with a mouth full of bagel. But these episodes are now the exception, not the rule of my life.

I want to share what's worked for me and for clients in my coaching practice—real, practical stuff based on science that actually helps in the real world. We'll cover:

- The different flavors of overthinking—from replaying embarrassing moments on mental repeat to creating disaster scenarios about things that haven't even happened (and probably never will). I call this last one "disaster porn," and it's my personal specialty!

- The anxiety-overthinking loop from hell. It's like a toxic relationship between two terrible roommates in your brain, each making the other worse.

- Why overthinking can be as addictive as scrolling through social media at 1 a.m. when you have an important meeting the next day. Your brain gets hooked on the "solving" sensation even when there's nothing to solve.

- How our poor, overtaxed brains are drowning in information overflow. No wonder we're all walking around like mental zombies half the time!

- Simple mindfulness practices that don't require you to become a monk or sit cross-legged for hours. (Though if that's your thing, rock on!)

- How to call BS on your own thoughts. This was HUGE for me—learning to say, "Thanks for sharing, brain, but that's actually ridiculous" when my mind tried to convince me everyone at the party was judging my laugh.

- Real talk about sleep, food, and exercise—because it's hard to have a chill mind when your body is running on energy drinks and panic.

- Practical strategies for when you feel yourself sliding back into overthink mode. Like that time I created a "worry appointment" for myself—scheduled worry time so my anxiety knew it would get its turn and could shut up until then. (Sounds crazy, worked amazingly well!)

I'll share plenty of my own embarrassing stories throughout—like when I almost canceled a trip to Italy because I convinced myself the Airbnb host secretly hated me based on their use of a period instead of an exclamation point. Or the time I rehearsed asking for a raise so many times that when the actual meeting came, I started with "As I've been practicing saying..." Smooth.

Look, I'm not some fancy expert with a wall of degrees. I'm just someone who got sick of living in my own head and found ways to break free. No big words, no complicated theories—just stuff that works in real life when you're freaking out about whether that text message your friend sent seemed "kind of short."

If you're exhausted from mental spin cycles, if you've ever found yourself googling "how to know if you're overthinking about overthinking," or if you just want to enjoy a movie without pausing it to analyze the subtle subtext of the main character's coffee order, this book is for you.

The version of you that isn't mentally exhausted all the time still exists. The you that can make a decision without creating seventeen contingency plans is in there somewhere. Let's go find that person together!

So, grab a drink (maybe not a mojito if you're like me and still slightly traumatized), get comfortable, and let's talk about how to tell your overactive brain to chill the hell out. Your future, well-rested, less-stressed self is going to be so grateful.

Turn the page. Your mind deserves a break!

Part 1:

Understanding Overthinking

Chapter 1:

What Is Overthinking?

Overthinking is when your thoughts get stuck on an endless hamster wheel, spinning round and round without getting anywhere useful. It's like having a hyperactive detective in your brain who refuses to close any case, ever. That work email you sent? Better analyze the tone for the seventeenth time! That weird look your friend gave you? Time to launch a full investigation into whether they secretly hate you!

Define Overthinking

So, what exactly is this mind monster I call overthinking? Let me paint you a picture.

It's Tuesday night, 2:17 a.m. You're wide awake, staring at the ceiling, mentally replaying that comment you made during the team meeting. "I should have phrased it differently," you think. "Everyone probably thought I was an idiot." Your brain helpfully supplies fourteen alternative versions of what you could have said instead. None of this will change what happened, but your mind doesn't care—it's committed to this late-night feature film of regret.

That, my friend, is overthinking in its natural habitat.

Overthinking comes in several delicious flavors, each with its own special way of making you miserable:

- **Rumination**: This is when your brain gets stuck replaying past events like a movie critic who watched the same bad film fifty times. My personal rumination record? Two weeks obsessing over calling my boss by the wrong name. (For the record, she didn't care and had forgotten by lunchtime.)

- **Excessive planning**: This is overthinking disguised as productivity. It's when you create seventeen contingency plans for a simple dinner party, including detailed scenarios for what you'll do if someone spills wine, brings an unexpected guest, or aliens invade during dessert.

- **Self-criticism**: This charming form of overthinking is when your inner voice turns into that mean girl from high school. Everything becomes evidence of your flaws. Forgot to buy milk? Obviously, you're a failure at basic adulting. Someone didn't text back immediately? Clearly, you're fundamentally unlikable.

- **Analysis paralysis**: When you've gathered so much information and considered so many angles that you've completely short-circuited your decision-making ability. This is how I ended up with 47 open browser tabs researching vacuum cleaners for six months while continuing to use a broken one that made sounds like a dying whale.

These forms often overlap and feed each other in what I call the "Mental Merry-Go-Round From Hell."

You start by ruminating about a mistake, which triggers self-criticism, which leads to excessive planning to "never let that happen again," which causes analysis paralysis because now you're overwhelmed, which gives you something new to ruminate about... and round we go!

The effects of this mental circus extend far beyond just feeling anxious.

Overthinking seeps into every corner of your life:

- **Personal effects**: The most immediate casualty is your peace of mind. Your brain never fully relaxes because it's always chewing on something. Sleep becomes elusive as your mind decides 3 a.m. is the perfect time to replay every embarrassing moment from your life. Your self-confidence takes a beating too—it's hard to feel self-assured when your brain is constantly second-guessing everything you do.

- **Career impact**: Overthinking can absolutely tank your professional life. Decisions take forever because you're considering every possible outcome (including ones that have a 0.0001% chance of happening). Emails sit in your drafts folder for days because you're rewriting them to eliminate any possible misinterpretation. Creative thinking suffers because your brain is too busy with unnecessary analysis to make new connections.

- **Effects on others**: Here's the part we often don't recognize—overthinking doesn't just torture us; it affects everyone around us. Your partner gets dragged into hour-long discussions about whether your friend's tone of voice meant she's secretly mad at you. Your kids learn that making decisions is a long, stressful process, rather than something that is sometimes simple and intuitive. Friends start introducing topics with "Don't overthink this, but..."

The good news? Recognizing these patterns is the first step to breaking free from them. And unlike some self-help books that make you feel like you need a personality transplant, the strategies we'll explore are designed for real humans with real, messy brains.

Psychological and Physiological Effects

I convinced myself I had a brain tumor because I had a headache for two days straight. I googled symptoms at 3 a.m. (rookie mistake), diagnosed myself with approximately seventeen fatal conditions, and drafted a mental will dividing my precious collection of mismatched coffee mugs among my loved ones. I even practiced my "brave face" in the mirror for when I'd break the news to my family.

The actual diagnosis when I finally dragged myself to the doctor? Dehydration and tension from—wait for it—stress and overthinking. The irony wasn't lost on me: I'd literally worried myself sick about being sick.

The Mental Mess

Overthinking creates a psychological tornado that tears through your emotional landscape:

- **Stress and anxiety**: These are overthinking's BFFs. Your body can't tell the difference between imagining a disaster and actually experiencing one. So, when you spend hours picturing worst-case scenarios, your body helpfully floods with stress hormones as if those scenarios were really happening.

- **Depression**: Overthinking and depression feed each other like two terrible roommates sharing bad habits. Ruminating on negative thoughts creates the perfect breeding ground for depression, which then gives you even more negative stuff to overthink.

- **Agitation and erratic behavior**: Ever snapped at someone because you were stuck in your head about something completely unrelated? *Raises hand sheepishly*. Overthinking puts your nervous system on high alert, making you jumpy, irritable, and about as pleasant to be around as a caffeinated raccoon.

- **Tanking self-esteem**: Overthinking is like having a full-time critic living in your head, pointing out every flaw and mistake with gleeful enthusiasm. After a while, you start believing the nasty reviews.

- **Decision paralysis**: When you overthink, even tiny choices become overwhelming. The mental cost-benefit analysis never ends, and you're left frozen like a deer in headlights.

The Body Battleground

While all this mental chaos is happening, your body is taking a beating too:

- **Brain changes**: Chronic overthinking actually rewires your brain, strengthening neural pathways that focus on threats and problems. It's like building a superhighway for negative thoughts while the positive thinking roads become overgrown with weeds.

- **Sleep disruption**: Ever tried to sleep while your brain is hosting the Overthinking Olympics? It's like trying to nap in the middle of a rock concert. Sleep disruption then leads to even more overthinking because your tired brain can't regulate emotions properly.

- **Immune system impacts**: Your immune system takes a serious hit when you're constantly overthinking. Those stress hormones I mentioned earlier? They suppress immune function when they stick around too long.

- **Digestion disasters**: The brain-gut connection is real. When your mind is in overdrive, your digestive system often goes haywire. Stomachaches, nausea, appetite changes—it's like your gut is staging a protest against your overthinking.

- **Muscle tension and pain**: All that mental stress gets stored in your body, creating tension that leads to headaches, back pain, and general achiness. My shoulders used to live somewhere up around my ears from holding so much tension. My massage therapist once asked if I was training to become a professional statue.

- **Heart health hazards**: The constant activation of your stress response isn't great for your heart. Increased blood pressure, elevated heart rate—it's like putting your cardiovascular system on a roller coaster it never asked to ride.

These effects aren't permanent. Your brain and body are remarkably resilient and can bounce back when you start breaking the overthinking cycle. I'm living proof—my blood pressure normalized, my sleep improved, and my immune system strengthened once I got my overthinking under control.

Common Myths about Overthinking

The other day, I saw this meme of a woman staring into space with the caption, "Me overthinking whether I locked the door even though I checked three times." Everyone in the comments was like, "OMG, so me!" and "I'm in this photo, and I don't like it!" Here's the thing, though—that's not overthinking. That's just having a normal brain fart.

Actual overthinking would be, "I think I locked the door, but what if I didn't? A burglar could break in. All our stuff would be stolen. We'd lose irreplaceable photos. Insurance might not cover everything. We'd have to move because I'd never feel safe again. My partner would resent me forever for ruining our lives with one careless mistake. This is proof I can't handle basic adult responsibilities..." And on and on until you're mentally rehearsing your divorce proceedings over a door you probably locked anyway.

See the difference?

Let's bust some common myths about overthinking that might be keeping you stuck in that mental hamster wheel:

Myth #1: Overthinking is just being forgetful or absentminded. Nope! Those moments when you can't remember where you put your phone (while talking on it) or walk into a room and forget why you're there are just normal brain glitches we all experience. They're usually caused by your attention being divided, not by overthinking. True overthinking is an active process of excessive, often repetitive thought that goes far beyond momentary confusion.

Myth #2: Overthinking is the same as careful planning. Oh, how I wish this were true! I've often justified my overthinking spirals as "just being thorough." But there's a massive difference between thoughtful preparation and overthinking.

Careful planning means considering relevant factors and making decisions based on the information available. Overthinking means getting stuck in analysis paralysis, considering increasingly unlikely scenarios, and never reaching a conclusion.

Myth #3: Smart people overthink more. This myth is particularly dangerous because it makes overthinking feel like a badge of honor. "I overthink because my brain is just so powerful and complex!"

While intelligence and overthinking can coexist, they're not the same thing. Some brilliant people make decisions quickly and confidently, while some average thinkers can get trapped in overthinking cycles.

Overthinking isn't using your intelligence—it's misusing it. It's like having a Ferrari but only driving it in tight circles in a parking lot. All that horsepower, going nowhere.

Myth #4: Overthinking helps prevent problems. This was my personal favorite myth for years. "If I think through every possible scenario, nothing can go wrong!"

The painful truth I had to accept? Overthinking often creates more problems than it solves. It increases anxiety, clouds judgment, and wastes mental energy on unlikely outcomes while potentially missing obvious solutions.

Myth #5: Overthinking and worrying are the same thing. While these two troublemakers often hang out together, they're not identical. Worrying is focused on specific concerns about the future, while overthinking can involve the past, present, or future and often includes excessive analysis rather than just anxiety.

All squares are rectangles, but not all rectangles are squares. Similarly, all worrying involves some overthinking, but not all overthinking is worry. When I spent three days analyzing exactly how my voice sounded during a presentation

I'd already given, that wasn't worry—it was pure, unproductive overthinking about something I couldn't change.

Myth #6: You can think your way out of overthinking. This is like trying to put out a fire by throwing more fire on it. You can't use the same overthinking patterns to solve your overthinking problem. That's just... more overthinking!

Trust me, I've tried. I once read a book about overthinking and then spent two weeks overthinking whether I was implementing the strategies correctly. The irony was completely lost on me at the time.

The truth is, breaking free from overthinking often requires stepping outside your usual thought patterns—something we'll explore in the coming chapters.

Chapter 2:

Why We Overthink

So there I was, standing in my kitchen at midnight, staring into my open refrigerator for the fourth time in an hour. I wasn't hungry. I wasn't even looking for anything specific.

I was just trying to distract myself from the endless loop playing in my head about whether I'd offended my friend earlier that day with an offhand comment about her new haircut.

"Did she seem quiet afterward? Was her laugh a little forced? Should I text her to apologize? But what if she didn't notice anything, and my text makes it weird? Maybe I should wait until tomorrow. But then what if she's been upset all night?"

As I finally closed the fridge door (sorry, electric bill), I had to ask myself, "Why do I *do* this to myself?"

The Perfect Storm: How Anxiety, Perfectionism, and Fear Keep the Overthinking Engine Running

I once spent three hours drafting a two-sentence email to decline a dinner invitation. THREE HOURS. I wrote version after version, analyzing each word choice, second-guessing the tone, and imagining how the recipient might interpret every possible variation.

"Sorry, I can't make it Friday" (too blunt?). "Unfortunately, I'm unable to attend" (too formal?). "I'd love to, but I'm already committed elsewhere" (but what if they ask where?).

By hour three, I was so mentally exhausted that I nearly canceled all my plans for the month just to avoid sending the damn email.

This is what happens when anxiety, perfectionism, and fear of failure throw a party in your brain.

Anxiety: The Overeager Security Guard

Anxiety is like having an overzealous security guard patrolling your mind. This guard means well—they're trying to protect you from threats—but they see danger *everywhere*.

"What's that? Someone didn't immediately respond to your text? Emergency! They must hate you now! Analyze every interaction you've had with them for the past year to figure out what you did wrong!"

The problem is that anxiety doesn't just warn you about legitimate threats; it treats everything as potentially dangerous. A slightly awkward conversation becomes a social catastrophe. A minor mistake at work becomes career suicide. That weird pain in your side? Definitely a rare tropical disease you read about once (never mind that you've never left your time zone).

When anxiety is running the show, your thoughts become a search party looking for problems—even when there aren't any to find. And because anxiety is never satisfied with simple answers, the search never ends. That's why you can spend hours trying to "solve" a problem that doesn't actually exist.

Perfectionism: The Impossible Dream

Ah, perfectionism. It sounds so positive, doesn't it? Who doesn't want to do things perfectly?

But perfectionism isn't about doing your best—it's about setting standards so impossibly high that you're guaranteed to fall short. It's like trying to drive to the moon in your Honda Civic. You're not going to make it, pal, no matter how determined you are.

Perfectionism fuels overthinking because it keeps moving the goalposts. Just when you think you've figured something out or made a decision, your inner perfectionist chimes in: "But is it the *best* decision? Is there a *better* way? Have you considered *every* possible angle?"

And so the mental hamster wheel keeps spinning. You keep searching for the perfect solution, the perfect response, the perfect plan—not realizing that "perfect" doesn't exist in the messy reality of human life.

Fear of Failure: The Dream Crusher

Fear of failure is the voice that whispers, "What if you mess this up? What if everyone sees you're not as competent as they thought? What if this is the mistake that finally exposes you as a fraud?"

This fear keeps you stuck in overthinking loops because it makes the stakes feel impossibly high for even minor decisions. When you're terrified of making the wrong choice, you'll analyze options until your brain turns to mush rather than risk being wrong.

Fear of the Unknown: The Uncertainty Allergy

Humans hate uncertainty. We'd rather know something bad is definitely going to happen than not know what's coming at all. This is why people will stay in unhappy situations rather than risk change—at least the current misery is familiar! When faced with uncertainty, your brain tries to create certainty through overthinking. If you can just think about all possible outcomes, maybe you can prepare for anything! (Spoiler alert: You can't.)

This is why you might lie awake the night before a job interview, mentally rehearsing answers to questions that will never be asked. Or why you might obsess over whether your new relationship will work out, creating elaborate scenarios of potential problems before you've even had your third date.

The Shadows That Follow Us: How Our Past Shapes Our Overthinking

Remember that time as a kid when someone laughed at your drawing, and now, twenty years later, you still feel that twist in your stomach when sharing your creative work? Or how about when your dad's constant criticism left you second-guessing every decision? These aren't just memories—they're active forces shaping how your brain processes information today.

Our minds don't develop in a vacuum. By the time we're adults, we've been molded by countless experiences, some so subtle we barely noticed them happening. Yet these experiences create the mental pathways we use every single day.

When Yesterday Crowds Out Today

Jake grew up with a mom who constantly worried about money. "Don't touch that, we can't afford to replace it!" was her daily refrain. Now, at 35, despite his comfortable salary, Jake agonizes over every purchase, running through worst-case scenarios for hours before buying even necessities.

His childhood programming runs deep, whispering, *Danger lurks in every financial decision.*

This is how the past hijacks the present. Those early lessons weren't just heard—they were absorbed into the very structure of Jake's thinking patterns.

Trauma Doesn't Just Go Away

"Just get over it" might be the least helpful advice ever given. Trauma isn't something we simply walk away from. Whether it's a single devastating event or years of subtle undermining, trauma rewires our brains.

Sarah survived a car accident at sixteen. Fifteen years later, she still maps out alternative routes to avoid the intersection where it happened. More significantly, she overthinks every travel plan, imagining disaster scenarios that keep her awake at night. Her brain is doing exactly what it was designed to do: Protect her from experiencing that pain again, even if the protection itself causes suffering.

The Cultural Blueprint

We don't just inherit genes from our families—we inherit ways of seeing the world. If you grew up in a household or culture where expressing emotions was considered weak, you might now overthink every feeling, analyzing whether it's "appropriate" to feel hurt, angry, or sad rather than simply experiencing the emotion.

Cultural influences extend beyond family, too. Growing up in a community that valued academic achievement above all else might leave you overthinking every professional choice through the narrow lens of status and credentials, missing opportunities that could bring genuine fulfillment.

Breaking Free Without Denying Your Story

Here's the tricky part: acknowledging these influences doesn't mean blaming your past for everything or feeling helpless about changing. It means understanding the source code that's running your mental programs.

Next time you catch yourself in an overthinking spiral, try asking, "Whose voice is this really? Mine today, or something echoing from my past?"

Sometimes, simply recognizing "This fear isn't about my current reality—it's my eight-year-old self's reaction" creates enough distance to loosen overthinking's grip.

Brain Traffic Jams: When Your Thoughts Can't Find the Exit

Have you ever driven through a roundabout several times because you missed your exit? Your thoughts do the exact same thing when you're overthinking.

Your Brain's Superhighways and Dirt Roads

Picture your brain as a big landscape crossed with countless roads. Some are eight-lane superhighways you've traveled a million times—like your route to work or your morning routine. Others are barely visible dirt paths you rarely use—like trying to remember high school calculus.

When you think a thought repeatedly, something remarkable happens: Your brain physically changes. The neural pathways—those roads your thoughts travel on—actually get wider and more efficient. It's like upgrading from a bumpy dirt road to a smooth highway.

This explains why it is so difficult to break free from overthinking. You've paved premium highways for your worry thoughts!

The Physical Reality of Mental Loops

"But it's just thinking," I hear you say. "How can thoughts physically change anything?"

The truth is, your thoughts aren't just abstract concepts floating in some mysterious mind-space. They're actual electrical signals traveling along physical cells called neurons. These neurons connect to each other through junctions called synapses (think of them as the intersections in our road analogy).

When you repeatedly worry about that embarrassing thing you said at last week's meeting, you're sending electrical traffic down the same neural route over and over. Your helpful brain, trying to be efficient, responds by strengthening that route.

This strengthening involves physical changes:

- Neurons grow more branches to connect with others.

- Synapses become more efficient at transmitting signals.

- Supporting cells multiply to maintain these busy highways.

- In scientific language, we call this "neuroplasticity," but I prefer "mental road construction."

Stuck in the Loop: The Brain's Default Mode

Ever notice how your mind wanders to the same worries during quiet moments? That's your brain's default mode network (DMN) at work. I just call it your "worry wanderer." This network activates when you're not focused on anything specific.

For overthinkers, the DMN often defaults to well-traveled worry highways. It's like your mental GPS is broken and keeps rerouting you through "Anxiety Avenue and Rumination Road."

Breaking the Loop: Creating New Roads

Here's the good news: You can build new mental highways. Better yet, those old worry roads will actually start to fade when unused, like paths in the woods growing over with weeds.

When you consciously direct your thoughts differently, you're literally carving new physical paths through your brain tissue. At first, it feels bumpy and requires effort—like driving on a rough trail instead of the familiar highway. But with repetition, these new constructive thought patterns become your brain's preferred routes.

The Science of Changing Your Mind

Let me share a little secret from neuroscience that changed my life: Neurons that fire together, wire together. This means whatever you practice strengthens in your brain.

Practice worrying? You get better at worrying. Practice calm responses. You get better at responding calmly.

It's that simple—and that difficult.

Your Brain's Incredible Power to Change

The most amazing thing about your brain is not its tendency to get stuck; it's its remarkable ability to unstick itself when given the right tools.

Every time you interrupt an overthinking loop, you're physically weakening that neural pathway. Every time you choose a different response, you're building a new, healthier route.

Your brain is always changing. The question is, are you directing that change, or are you overthinking on autopilot? Those thought loops aren't just habits; they're actual physical structures in your brain. And anything physical can be changed with the right approach and a bit of persistence.

Mind Traffic Jam: How Modern Life Overwhelms Your Mental Highway

Remember when you had to wait for the evening news to find out what happened in the world? When work emails couldn't reach you at the dinner table? When "following" someone meant physically walking behind them rather than getting updates about their breakfast choices?

Those days are gone, my friend. And while I'm not suggesting we return to carrier pigeons and typewriters, our brains are paying a steep price for our always-connected modern existence.

Your Poor Brain: Designed for Lions, Dealing With Notifications

Our brains evolved during simpler times when the main concerns were "Is that a lion?" and "Where can I find food?" Today, that same ancient hardware is processing an estimated 34GB of information daily, equivalent to about 174 newspapers' worth of content. Every. Single. Day.

No wonder you're overthinking! Your mental processing center is working overtime without hazard pay.

The Bottomless Scroll: Social Media's Mind Trap

Each time you scroll through social media, your brain gets tiny hits of dopamine—the feel-good chemical that keeps you coming back for more.

But along with those little pleasure zaps comes a barrage of information your brain feels compelled to process:

- Your cousin's political rants.

- Your colleague's perfect vacation photos (that make your last staycation look like solitary confinement).

- Breaking news alerts about disasters halfway around the world.

- Targeted ads reminding you of products you don't need but suddenly want.

- And all this happens while a little voice whispers, "Everyone else has their life together. Why don't you?"

That's why heavy social media users experience more rumination and overthinking. Your brain never gets the signal that it's caught up on processing all the input.

The Work-Life Blur: When Your Brain Can't Clock Out

Remember offices? Those buildings we used to leave at the end of the workday? Now our homes have become our offices, our phones keep us tethered to work 24-7, and the average employee checks work emails 74 times a day (Evans, 2014). Yes, you read that correctly—74 times!

When your brain can't distinguish between work time and rest time, it remains in problem-solving mode constantly. That spreadsheet issue follows you to the dinner table. That client email haunts your shower thoughts. Your brain never fully disengages from work puzzles, creating perfect conditions for overthinking.

News Cycle Nausea: When Information Becomes Toxic

In the past, news cycles moved at human speed. Today, they operate at algorithm speed.

The constant stream of (mostly negative) news triggers our threat-detection systems repeatedly. Your brain, being the helpful worrier it is, thinks, "Danger! I must keep thinking about this problem until it's solved!"

But here's the kicker: Most news stories highlight problems you personally cannot solve. So, your brain keeps spinning its wheels, analyzing threats it can't address, creating the perfect overthinking storm.

Digital Amnesia: When Google Becomes Your Memory

Why remember anything when you can Google it? While convenient, our outsourced memory has consequences.

Knowing information is readily available online makes us less likely to commit it to memory.

The downside? Your brain gets less practice at information processing and retrieval, making it more likely to get stuck in overthinking loops when faced with problems.

Understanding how modern life overwhelms your brain is the first step toward relief. Your overthinking isn't a personal failure; it's a natural response to an unnatural information environment.

Chapter 3:

The Consequences of Overthinking

You've probably heard that classic joke about the overthinking mind: "My brain has too many tabs open, and I don't know which one is playing music." We laugh because it's true, but what happens when those tabs never close? When does the mental music ever stop?

The Emotional Hangover: When Your Mind Drinks Too Much Worry

Remember the last time you woke up after too many glasses of wine? That foggy head, the sensitivity to everything, the general feeling that the world is a bit too much today? Welcome to the emotional hangover of overthinking—except this one doesn't clear up after a greasy breakfast and two aspirin.

The Anxiety Spiral

Overthinking and anxiety are like toxic best friends who bring out the worst in each other. Your overthinking mind says, "Hey, let's consider every possible thing that could go wrong!" Then anxiety chimes in: "Great idea! And let's feel all of those disasters happening right now!"

Before you know it, you're sitting perfectly safe in your living room while experiencing the emotional equivalent of falling from an airplane without a parachute.

What's actually happening is that your body can't tell the difference between real threats and imagined ones. Each worry thought triggers the same stress response as if you were facing actual danger. No wonder you feel exhausted, you're emotionally running from tigers all day long while physically sitting at your desk.

The Confidence Thief

Nothing steals self-esteem quite like overthinking. It's like having a hypercritical roommate who follows you everywhere:

- "Should you really wear that?"

- "Remember that slightly awkward thing you said three years ago? Everyone else does."

- "They're probably just being nice to you because they pity you."

This constant self-questioning erodes your confidence until making even small decisions feels overwhelming. I once spent forty-five minutes deciding whether to order the chicken or fish at a restaurant. By the time I ordered, I wasn't even hungry anymore. The waiter probably thought I was writing a doctoral thesis on menu options.

The Short Fuse Phenomenon

Ever notice how the more you overthink, the shorter your temper gets? There's a reason for that. Overthinking burns through your mental resources like a teenager burns through data when the Wi-Fi goes down.

When your mental energy is depleted from hours of circular thinking, you have less capacity to handle normal frustrations. The person who cuts you off in traffic isn't just inconsiderate; they become the physical manifestation of everything wrong with humanity.

Your partner leaving dishes in the sink isn't a minor annoyance; it's clear evidence that they don't value your feelings or respect your home. At least, that's how it feels when your emotional reserves are drained from overthinking.

The Desperation Decision-Making

Perhaps most dangerous is how overthinking can lead to poor choices made from a place of desperation. When you've analyzed a problem from every possible angle, your mind craves resolution—any resolution.

This explains why overthinkers sometimes make impulsive decisions that seem completely out of character. After weeks of deliberating whether to stay in a job, you might suddenly quit without any backup plan. After months of analyzing relationship problems, you might make a major relationship decision based on a minor disagreement.

It's like being lost in a maze for hours and then deciding to just smash through the nearest wall. At least it's doing something.

The Prison of Your Own Making

The cruelest irony? Overthinking convinces you that more thinking is the solution, trapping you in an endless loop. You feel stuck inside your own head, watching life happen from behind glass while you try to figure it all out first.

The good news? This prison has a door, and you already have the key. In the coming chapters, we'll explore practical ways to step out of the overthinking trap and back into your life, not because you've solved all your problems, but because you've learned how to carry them differently. Your thoughts may feel like facts, but they're really just mental weather—constantly changing, sometimes stormy, but always passing through if you don't try to hold on to them.

When Your Body Pays the Bill: The Physical Cost of Mental Loops

Ever noticed how your shoulders creep up toward your ears during a particularly intense overthinking session? Or how does your jaw feel like you've been secretly moonlighting as a nutcracker? Your body keeps the score of your thought patterns, and unfortunately, it doesn't offer forgiveness for mental overdrafts.

The Stress Response That Never Clocks Out

Your body's stress response was designed for short bursts of action, like running from a predator or fighting off a threat. It was never meant to stay activated for the eight consecutive hours you spend worrying about that comment your boss made last Tuesday.

When overthinking keeps your stress response permanently switched on, your body pumps out cortisol and adrenaline like they're going out of style. These hormones are great for helping you escape a burning building, not so great when they're flooding your system while you're just sitting at your desk replaying conversations in your head.

The Exhaustion That Sleep Can't Fix

"But I got eight hours of sleep last night!" you protest to your reflection as dark circles stubbornly remain under your eyes. The problem? Overthinking creates a quality of sleep that's about as restful as napping on a roller coaster. Your body might be in bed, but your mind is running the Boston Marathon.

You fall asleep rehearsing tomorrow's presentation, wake up at 3 a.m. wondering if you offended someone five years ago, and then spend the pre-alarm hour mentally redecorating your living room.

No wonder you're tired. Your brain hasn't had a break since 2017.

From Headaches to Heart Disease: The Longer-Term Fallout

Those tension headaches that have become your faithful afternoon companions? They're the tip of the iceberg. Chronic overthinking contributes to serious health issues that take years to develop but minutes to diagnose:

- **Heart disease**: Turns out, your heart doesn't appreciate being kept on high alert 24-7.

- **High blood pressure**: Your blood vessels can only take so much stress-induced constriction.

- **Diabetes**: Stress hormones mess with blood sugar regulation like a toddler messes with your organized drawers.

- **Compromised immune function**: Your body's defense system gets too tired fighting imaginary tigers to deal with actual viruses.

I'm not sharing this to scare you—well, maybe a little healthy fear is good—but to connect dots you might not have connected yourself. That chronic health issue you've been trying to solve with diet changes and medication?

Your overthinking habit might be the silent saboteur.

The Cognitive Catch

Here's a cruel irony: Overthinking actually makes you worse at thinking. It's like revving your car engine in park until you run out of gas.

When your brain is overwhelmed by circular thoughts, your working memory suffers, your attention scatters, and your decision-making abilities would make a Magic 8-Ball look reliable. "Ask again later" becomes your default response to even the simplest questions.

The Lifestyle Spiral

Then there's the domino effect on your daily habits. When you're mentally exhausted from overthinking:

- **Exercise feels impossible:** Who has the energy to run when they've been mentally running all day?.

- **Healthy eating requires too many decisions:** Frozen pizza requires zero thought, which feels like blessed relief.

- **Screen time increases:** Scrolling doesn't require mental energy from your already depleted reserves.

Before you know it, you've gained fifteen pounds, your muscles have forgotten what movement feels like, and your relationship with your couch has become more committed than most marriages.

Breaking the Body-Mind Feedback Loop

The good news? This physical toll isn't a one-way street. Just as your thoughts affect your body, your body can influence your thoughts. Sometimes the fastest way to break an overthinking spiral is through physical intervention—a brisk walk, deep breathing, or even just standing up and stretching. We'll explore these bodily escape hatches from overthinking in later chapters.

For now, simply noticing how your body responds to your thought patterns can be illuminating. That tension headache might actually be your body's way of waving a red flag: "Hello? Overthinking alert! Anyone listening down there?"

Love and Overthink: When Your Head Gets in the Way of Your Heart

Remember that time you sent a text message and got a simple "ok" in response? If you're an overthinker, that two-letter word probably launched a feature-length movie in your mind starring you as the villain who somehow ruined everything. Meanwhile, the sender was probably just busy or driving.

The Romantic Relationship Tax

In romantic relationships, overthinking acts like an unwelcome third wheel—one that shows up uninvited and hogs all the attention.

Take Sofia and Mikelson. When Mikelson said he needed space after an argument, Sofia's overthinking transformed "I need thirty minutes to cool down" into "He's planning his escape, probably consulting divorce lawyers, and I'll die alone with seventeen cats."

By the time Mikelson returned, ready to talk calmly, Sofia had already rehearsed twenty different breakup scenarios and was emotionally exhausted. Overthinkers often create problems that don't exist, then solve those imaginary problems with real emotions. The result? Partners who feel they can't win: "If I say something, it gets overthought. If I say nothing, my silence gets overthought."

The cruel paradox is that while overthinking stems from caring deeply, it can make you seem emotionally unavailable. Your body is present, but your mind is busy analyzing the relationship rather than experiencing it.

Parent-Child Complications

If you're a parent who overthinks, you might find yourself stuck in planning mode instead of playing mode. Your child asks to go to the park, and while you're calculating sun exposure risks and evaluating the likelihood of playground injuries, childhood is happening without you.

Or perhaps you're the adult child of an overthinker. You call with exciting news, only to have your parent immediately jump to all the potential downsides of your opportunity. Their anxiety masquerades as concern, but it lands as a lack of faith in your abilities.

I once spent so long researching the "perfect" birthday gift for my nephew that I missed the ordering deadline entirely. Nothing says "happy birthday" like a belated present and an aunt who can tell you the pros and cons of every toy on the market!

Friendship Friction

Friendships should be our safe harbors, but overthinking can turn them into anxiety-producing territories. Consider these common scenarios:

- You analyze a friend's tone in a group chat until you're convinced they're mad at you, leading to awkward interactions based on a problem that doesn't exist.

- You decline invitations because you're overthinking what to wear, what to say, or how you'll be perceived.

- You hesitate to reach out because "they probably don't want to hear from me," creating actual distance from imagined rejection.

Before you know it, friendship becomes another source of stress rather than support.

Extended Family Dynamics

Extended family relationships—with their historical baggage and intermittent contact—create perfect overthinking conditions. After the annual holiday gathering, you might spend weeks dissecting Aunt Martha's comment about your career choice or Uncle Bob's question about your love life.

These overthinking spirals are particularly frustrating because you might only see these family members once or twice a year, yet they can occupy mental real estate for months.

Breaking the Cycle

The common thread across all these relationships? Overthinking keeps you in your head when connection requires presence. While you're busy analyzing the relationship, you're missing opportunities to actually experience it.

Small changes can make big differences:

- Ask for clarification instead of assuming meaning.

- Share your overthinking tendencies with loved ones so they understand your process.

- Set a time limit on how long you'll mull over interactions.

Remember: most people don't analyze your words and actions with the intensity you apply to theirs. That "ok" text probably just means "ok"—nothing more, nothing less.

The Career Quicksand: When Overthinking Sinks Your Professional Life

Remember the last time you spent forty-five minutes crafting a two-sentence email? Or when you had three different browser tabs open researching the "perfect" approach to a simple task that should have taken fifteen minutes? Welcome to the professional consequences of overthinking—where careers move at the speed of second-guessing.

The Paradox of Paralysis

Here's the great irony of overthinking at work: It masquerades as thoroughness while actually tanking your productivity. You think you're being diligent by considering every angle of that proposal, but meanwhile, your colleague, who thinks at a normal human speed, has already submitted their work, gotten feedback, made improvements, and is now happily scrolling through vacation rentals while you're still perfecting paragraph three.

I once spent so long deliberating over the font for a presentation that I missed the actual deadline for submitting the content. True story. My boss was not impressed with my extensive knowledge of serif versus sans-serif typography.

The "I Don't Wanna" Syndrome

Overthinking creates a particularly nasty form of procrastination—one where you're mentally exhausted before you even begin. When every task feels like it requires Olympic-level mental gymnastics, suddenly organizing your sock drawer seems like a compelling alternative to starting that report.

This "I don't want to" syndrome isn't laziness; it's your brain's reasonable rebellion against the unnecessarily complicated approach you've taken to work. It's like your mind is saying, "If we're going to make this simple task into a doctoral dissertation, I'd rather check out entirely."

Decision Fatigue: The Silent Career Killer

Every decision you make drains a little mental energy. Overthinkers burn through their daily decision allowance before lunch, leaving them in a state of mental fog precisely when critical thinking is most needed.

By 3 p.m., simple questions like "Should I respond to this email now or later?" feel as complicated as solving advanced calculus. This decision fatigue leads to one of two problematic outcomes: either avoiding decisions entirely (creating bottlenecks) or making hasty, poor choices just to be done with the matter (creating mistakes).

Neither impresses your boss.

The Burnout Expressway

While your coworkers take the normal road to their career destinations, overthinking puts you on an express lane to burnout. Every project becomes an endurance test, every email an exercise in anxiety, and every meeting a potential minefield of saying the wrong thing. No wonder you're exhausted by Wednesday afternoon. You're not just doing your job; you're doing your job plus running a continuous mental simulation of everything that could possibly go wrong.

The Real-World Consequences

Overthinking at work isn't just annoying; it can derail your career in tangible ways:

- **Missed deadlines:** Because perfect is the enemy of done.

- **Strained work relationships:** As colleagues get frustrated waiting for your input.

- **Poor performance reviews:** When your output doesn't match your capabilities.

- **Passed-over promotions:** As decisive colleagues advance while you deliberate.

- **Disciplinary actions:** When procrastination finally catches up with you.

I had a friend who was brilliant at her job but nearly got fired because her overthinking led to consistent delays in project completion. Her boss interpreted her perfectionism as a lack of commitment rather than what it really was—analysis paralysis.

Part 2:

Breaking Free from the Overthinking Trap

Chapter 4:

Awareness Is the First Step

If you've made it this far, congratulations! You've already done something many overthinkers never do—acknowledge that those endless mental loops aren't actually helping you. That's huge. Seriously. Give yourself a moment to appreciate that first step.

Now comes the part where we get personal, where we turn the spotlight from overthinking in general to overthinking in your life specifically. Don't worry; this isn't where I ask you to lie on a couch and talk about your childhood (though if that helps, go ahead and get comfortable). This is about becoming a detective in your own life, investigating the specific ways overthinking shows up for you.

Getting to Know Your Overthinking Habits

You can't fix what you don't understand. Think about it like this: If your car starts making a weird noise, you need to figure out what's causing it before you can repair it. Your overthinking works the same way.

Self-awareness is your flashlight in the dark room of your thoughts. Without it, you're just bumping into furniture and stubbing your mental "toes." When you shine that light on your thinking patterns, suddenly you can see what's actually there instead of what your anxious mind imagines.

Remember those first three chapters? Now's the time to put them to work. Grab a notebook (yes, an actual one—your phone has too many distractions), find a quiet spot, and let's play detective with your own mind.

Start by asking yourself, *How often do I actually overthink throughout the day?* Be honest—no judging yourself here. Is it five times? Twenty? Are we talking constant background noise or occasional thought spirals?

I used to overthink so much that my partner once asked if I was rehearsing for a debate while I was brushing my teeth. Turns out, I was mentally arguing with my boss about something that hadn't even happened yet. Talk about productive use of toothbrush time!

Next, track how long these thinking loops last. Five minutes? An hour? Do they follow you to bed and become uninvited guests in your dreams? Understanding the duration helps you recognize just how much of your life these thought loops are stealing.

What themes keep popping up? Work stress? Relationship worries? That embarrassing thing you said at a party in 2017? Our brains have favorite grooves they like to get stuck in—identify yours.

The gold mine of this exercise is spotting your triggers. Does checking social media send you into comparison spirals? Do certain people activate your insecurity button? Maybe Sunday evenings trigger Monday dread? Knowing your triggers is like having an early warning system.

My friend, Jamie, discovered that every time her phone rang unexpectedly, she'd spiral into catastrophic thinking. Once she recognized this trigger, she could prepare a quick mental response: "It's just a phone call, not an emergency."

This detective work isn't always comfortable. You might discover thought patterns you've been running from. That's okay. Actually, it's great because now you can see the cage you've built around yourself, and you can't escape a cage you don't know exists.

Try this: Carry a small notebook for a week. When you catch yourself overthinking, jot down the time, the topic, how long it lasted, and what might have triggered it. Don't try to stop it yet—just observe like you're watching someone else's mind. This distance alone can be revolutionary.

Self-awareness isn't about judging yourself harshly. It's about becoming curious about your mind's habits. Think of yourself as a scientist studying an interesting specimen, which happens to be your own brain.

Breaking the overthinking cycle starts with this honest look in the mirror. You can't change what you don't acknowledge. Simply noticing your patterns has already started weakening their hold on you. Awareness itself is the first crack in the overthinking prison walls.

Overthinking Bootcamp: Your Personal Toolkit for Mental Clarity

Imagine your brain is like a hyperactive puppy. It needs training, patience, and sometimes a gentle redirect. These exercises aren't about silencing your thoughts; they're about becoming the confident dog trainer of your own mind.

Journaling

Grab a notebook that makes you smile. Seriously, if cute unicorns or sleek leather binding motivate you to write, go for it. The goal? Dump your thoughts onto paper like you're cleaning out an overstuffed closet.

Try this: Every morning or evening, write for 10 minutes without stopping. No editing, no judging. Just pure, unfiltered brain vomit. You'll be surprised what patterns emerge.

I once discovered I was overthinking work presentations three weeks before they even happened. Talk about unnecessary stress!

Mindfulness

Mindfulness sounds fancy, but it's really just paying attention to the present moment. Close your eyes right now. Take a deep breath. Notice how your body feels. Hear the sounds around you. When a thought tries to hijack your attention, gently—and I mean gently—guide it back.

Pro tip: Start with five-minute sessions. Your mind will wander. That's normal. It's like trying to teach a toddler to sit still—frustrating but possible with practice.

Timed Overthinking

This might sound counterintuitive, but hear me out. Schedule specific "overthinking time." Give yourself 15 minutes a day to worry, analyze, and spiral. When the timer goes off, you're done. It's like putting your anxious thoughts in a timeout.

One of my support group members called this her "worry appointment." She'd literally put it in her calendar: 4:30 p.m. Overthinking Session. After that? Thoughts, you're dismissed!

Setting Boundaries

Boundaries aren't just for relationships; they're for your brain too. Learn to say no to conversations, situations, and even your own thoughts that drain your energy. It's okay to tell your brain, "Not now, we've got better things to do."

Opening Up

Talking about your overthinking with trusted friends or a counselor is like releasing pressure from a steam valve. You don't need to solve everything; sometimes, just speaking your fears out loud makes them shrink.

Goal-Setting

Break big worries into tiny, manageable steps. Instead of "I'm a total failure," try "I'll send one job application this week." Small wins build confidence faster than you can say "self-doubt."

These exercises aren't about perfection. Some days, you'll nail them. Other days, your brain will feel like a chaotic mess. That's completely okay. Progress isn't linear; it's more like a drunk person trying to walk a straight line.

Your Journaling Roadmap

Forget everything you know about "perfect" journaling. This isn't about writing a Pulitzer Prize-winning novel. This is about getting brutally honest with yourself—messy handwriting, random tangents, and all.

The Thought Detective Prompts

Grab a notebook that makes you happy.

1. **The worry excavation:** Write down your current top three worries. Then ask yourself:

    o How likely is this worry to actually happen?

    o What's the worst-case scenario?

- o What's the best-case scenario?

- o What's most likely to happen?

2. **Thought pattern safari:** Track your thoughts like you're a wildlife researcher:

    - o What triggered this thought?

    - o How does this thought make my body feel?

    - o How long have I been carrying this thought?

    - o Is this thought helpful or harmful?

3. **The emotional weather report:** Describe your emotional state like a meteorologist:

    - o What's the current emotional temperature?

    - o Are there any storm warnings (big emotions)?

    - o What's causing this emotional climate?

Reflection Techniques That Actually Work

The 5-Minute Brain Dump

Set a timer for five minutes. Write everything that comes to mind without stopping or editing. No judgment, no filter.

It's like giving your brain a good shake and seeing what falls out.

The Conversation Replay

After a challenging interaction, write out

- what actually happened.

- what you're telling yourself happened.

- the difference between these two stories.

The Gratitude Hack

Every day, write three things you're grateful for. But here's the twist: They have to be specific. Not "I'm grateful for my family," but "I'm grateful my sister made me laugh so hard at dinner I snorted soda out of my nose."

Pro Overthinker Tips

- Some days, you'll write novels. On other days, you'll manage a single sentence. Both are victories.

- Your journal is your judgment-free zone. No one else needs to read this.

- If writing feels hard, try voice notes or typing on your phone.

- Consistency matters more than perfection.

Your brain is not your enemy. It's just trying to protect you, sometimes a bit too enthusiastically. Journaling is your way of saying, "Thanks for looking out for me, but I've got this."

Ready to start your thought treasure hunt?

Chapter 5:

Challenging the Thoughts

Remember when you were a kid and believed there was a monster under your bed? No matter how many times your parents checked, you just knew it was there, waiting for them to leave.

Then one day, you finally worked up the courage to look for yourself and found nothing but dust bunnies and a missing sock.

Your overthinking works exactly like that childhood monster. It's scary, it seems real, and it keeps you up at night. But when you shine a light on it and really look? It's mostly just dusty old fears wearing a scary mask.

Here's the thing about our brains: They're fantastic storytellers. They spin tales about who we are, what others think of us, and what we're capable of achieving. The problem? Many of these stories are complete fiction.

- "I'm not smart enough for this job."

- "Everyone at the party will think I'm awkward."

- "I always mess up important things."

- "They're only being nice because they feel sorry for me."

Sound familiar? These thoughts aren't facts; they're interpretations. Often, they're deeply flawed interpretations based on fears, past experiences, or things others have told us during vulnerable moments.

Identifying Cognitive Distortions

Your brain is like that friend who's always got some wild gossip to share. The problem is, half the time they've got their facts completely wrong.

Those irrational thoughts buzzing around your head have a fancy name in psychology circles—cognitive distortions. But let's call them what they really are: mind tricks. Your brain is playing pranks on you. The good news? Once you can spot these tricks, they lose a lot of their power.

The Most Wanted List of Mind Tricks

All-or-Nothing Thinking

This is black-and-white thinking with no gray area. Either you're a complete success or a total failure.

"I made one mistake in my presentation, so the whole thing was a disaster."

Reality check: Life happens in shades of gray. One mistake doesn't erase everything else you did well.

Fortune Telling

When you predict the future, somehow it's always terrible.

"If I ask her out, she'll definitely say no and probably laugh about it with her friends."

Reality check: Unless you've developed psychic powers (in which case, we need to talk about lottery numbers), you don't know what will happen.

Mind Reading

You're convinced you know what others are thinking, usually about you, and usually bad.

"My boss didn't smile at me this morning. She must be planning to fire me."

Reality check: People have their own stuff going on that has nothing to do with you. Maybe she just had a fight with her teenager or spilled coffee on her favorite shirt.

Catastrophizing

Taking a small problem and turning it into a five-alarm disaster.

"I forgot to respond to that email. My career is over."

Reality check: Most problems are fixable speed bumps, not life-ending sinkholes.

Emotional Reasoning

Believing that if you feel something, it must be true.

"I feel like an impostor, so I must be one."

Reality check: Feelings aren't facts. They're just your brain's interpretation of what's happening.

How to Catch Yourself in the Act

The tricky part about these mind games? They happen so automatically that they feel completely normal and true.

Here's how to become a thought detective:

1. **Get curious, not furious:** When you notice anxiety or stress rising, pause and ask, "What am I telling myself right now?" Be curious about your thoughts rather than immediately believing them.

2. **Write it down:** There's something powerful about seeing your thoughts on paper. Often, they look different and less convincing when they're outside your head.

3. **The evidence test:** Ask yourself, "What actual evidence do I have that this thought is true? What evidence do I have that it's not true?" Like a good detective, gather facts from both sides.

4. **The friend test:** Would you say this thought to a friend in your situation? If not, why are you saying it to yourself?

5. **The so-what game:** Follow your thought to its logical conclusion. "So, what if this happens? Then what? And then what?" Often, you'll find that even if your fear comes true, you'll handle it.

I caught myself in a classic mind trick last week. After a typo in an important email, I spiraled into "I'm so careless, they'll think I'm unprofessional, I'll lose credibility forever." When I wrote it down, I had to laugh. One typo = career death? Even for an overthinker like me, that was a stretch.

Your thoughts are not facts—they're just thoughts. Sometimes they're helpful, sometimes they're wildly off-base.

Your job isn't to stop having these thoughts (impossible) but to get better at recognizing when your brain is playing tricks on you.

So, ready to start catching your brain in the act?

Reframing Overthinking

Ever watched someone skilled in martial arts use an opponent's momentum against them? That's exactly what we're going to learn to do with your overthinking. Instead of fighting those thoughts head-on (and getting exhausted in the process), you'll learn to redirect their energy.

The Question Everything Approach

Remember how annoying four-year-olds are with their endless "why" questions? Channel that energy! When a negative thought pops up, hit it with questions:

- "Where's the actual evidence for this?"

- "Am I confusing feelings with facts?"

- "What would I tell my best friend if they had this thought?"

- "Is this thought helpful or just making me feel worse?"

- "What's another way to look at this situation?"

I once spent three days convinced a friend was mad at me because she didn't reply to my text. My brain constructed an elaborate story about how I'd offended her.

When I finally questioned this belief, I remembered she was on a camping trip with spotty cell service. Overthinking: 0, Reality: 1.

The Courtroom Method

Pretend you're a lawyer presenting evidence in a case. Your negative thought is the prosecution's claim. Your job? Be the defense attorney.

Prosecution: "Everyone at work thinks I'm incompetent."

Defense: "Your Honor, the evidence shows three colleagues specifically thanked me last week. My boss gave me positive feedback on my last project. One mistake doesn't define my entire professional reputation."

The key is being fair, not dismissing all negative thoughts, but not accepting them without evidence either.

Thought Experiments That Work

The Time-Travel Test

Ask yourself, "Will this matter in a week? A month? A year?" Most overthinking focuses on things that won't even register on your radar in the near future.

The Compassion Flip

When your inner critic goes wild, imagine it's speaking to someone you love. Would you let anyone talk to your friend that way? Probably not. So, why accept it for yourself?

The Percentage Game

Instead of all-or-nothing thinking ("This will definitely fail"), assign realistic percentages: "There's maybe a 20% chance this goes badly, which means there's an 80% chance it goes fine or even great."

A Quick Word on CBT and Friends

Cognitive behavioral therapy might sound fancy, but it's basically what we're doing here: examining the connection between thoughts and feelings, then changing the thoughts to improve the feelings. We'll deeply discuss CBT techniques in the next chapter, along with mindfulness practices and emotional reasoning strategies.

For now, remember this: Your thoughts are just thoughts. They're like weather: sometimes sunny, sometimes stormy, but always changing. You don't have to believe every thought that pops into your head.

My Favorite Reframing Tool

When I catch myself in an overthinking spiral, I use what I call the "So What" method. I follow my fear to its conclusion.

"What if I bomb this presentation?"

- "So, what? People might think I'm nervous."

- "So, what? They'll probably forget about it by tomorrow."

- "So, what? Even if they remember, one bad presentation doesn't define my career."

Each "so what" takes the power away from the fear until it shrinks to its actual size, usually much smaller than it first appeared. Remember, getting good at reframing takes practice. Your brain has been running these thought patterns for years. Be patient with yourself as you learn these new mental moves. We'll build on these foundations in the next chapter with more advanced techniques.

Developing Healthier Inner Dialogue

Imagine sharing your living space with someone who follows you everywhere, commenting on everything you do:

- "That outfit makes you look terrible."

- "Why did you say that? Everyone thinks you're an idiot now."

- "You'll never get this right. Why even try?"

You'd probably kick this roommate out, right? Yet most of us let this voice—our inner critic—live rent-free in our heads 24-7.

Meet Your Inner Critics and Cheerleaders

We all have multiple voices in our heads. No, I'm not suggesting you need psychiatric help! These voices are simply different parts of our thinking patterns:

- **The drill sergeant:** Harsh, demanding, never satisfied. "That's not good enough! Do it again!"

- **The catastrophizer:** Always predicting doom. "If this meeting goes badly, your career is over!"

- **The perfectionist:** Nothing is ever quite right. "99% is basically failing."

- **The compassionate friend:** Kind, understanding, and encouraging. "You're doing your best with what you have."

- **The wise observer:** Sees the bigger picture. "This is hard right now, but it's just one moment in a much larger story."

The problem isn't having these voices; it's which ones we let dominate.

Self-Criticism vs. Self-Compassion: The Ultimate Showdown

Let's clear up a big misconception: Self-compassion is not self-indulgence. It's not about giving yourself a pass to do whatever you want without consequences. Self-criticism says, "You're so lazy! What's wrong with you?" Self-compassion says, "This is difficult, and you're struggling right now. What do you need to take the next small step?"

Self-criticism says, "Everyone else can handle this. You're just weak." Self-compassion says, "Many people find this challenging. Being human means sometimes finding things hard."

Here's the plot twist: Research consistently shows that self-compassion motivates us more effectively than self-criticism (Godkin, 2020). Think about it, who would you work harder for? A boss who berates and insults you or one who believes in you while holding you to high standards?

Your Inner Voice Makeover

Ready to renovate that inner dialogue? Here's your toolkit:

Notice the Voice

You can't change what you don't notice. Start by simply observing your inner chatter without judgment. "Ah, there's my inner critic again."

Name the Voice

When you catch harsh self-talk, label it, "That's not me; that's my perfectionist talking." This creates instant distance and perspective.

Talk Back (Respectfully)

When your inner critic says, "You always mess things up," respond with, "Actually, that's not true. Remember when I handled that situation last month?"

Speak in the Third Person

Instead of "I'm so stupid," try "Sally, you're feeling frustrated right now." This simple shift reduces emotional reactivity.

The Golden Question

When you're struggling, ask yourself, "What would I say to a friend in this situation?" Then offer yourself the same kindness.

I used to have an inner voice that sounded suspiciously like my seventh-grade math teacher: critical, impatient, and convinced I'd never "get it." When I started noticing this voice, I realized how much unnecessary suffering it caused me. Now, when it appears, I thank it for trying to protect me (because that's often what the critical voice thinks it's doing), and then I choose a more helpful perspective.

Remember, the goal isn't to eliminate negative thoughts. It's to build a healthier relationship with all your thoughts. Some days, your inner critic will be louder than others. That's okay. With practice, your compassionate voice will get stronger and more automatic.

Your mind is like a neighborhood. You can't control who moves in, but you can choose who you invite over for coffee.

Chapter 6:

The Power of Presence

By now, you've discovered how your thoughts can hijack your life, dragging you backward into regrets or catapulting you forward into worst-case scenarios. Meanwhile, life itself happens right now, in this moment, often without you noticing.

The frantic pace of modern living doesn't help. Between pinging notifications, packed schedules, and the pressure to always be "on," we rarely settle fully into the now. Instead, we operate on autopilot—physically present but mentally elsewhere, rehearsing tomorrow's presentation or replaying last week's argument while stirring dinner.

But here's the thing about overthinking: It can only thrive when we abandon the present. Think about it—have you ever overthought something while being completely absorbed in the moment? Probably not.

Snap Back to Now: Mindfulness Techniques That Actually Work

Let's be honest—when was the last time your mind was actually where your body was? This morning, while brushing your teeth, were you mentally rehearsing your presentation? Or during lunch, did you replay that awkward conversation from yesterday?

So, how do we train our wandering minds to stay put? Enter mindfulness: your personal teleportation device back to reality.

The 5-4-3-2-1 Grounding Technique

When your thoughts are spiraling, try naming:

- 5 things you can see right now.

- 4 things you can touch.

- 3 things you can hear.

- 2 things you can smell (or like to smell).

- 1 thing you can taste.

I tried this during a particularly brutal overthinking episode before a job interview.

By the time I reached "taste," I had completely broken the thought loop and remembered I was just a person sitting in a car, not a collection of imagined failures.

The "Name That Thought" Practice

When a thought pops up, simply label it: "Planning thought." "Worry thought." "Memory thought." Then watch it float away.

This one makes me laugh because I've caught myself with some ridiculous categories: "Catastrophic thought where somehow I end up living in a cardboard box because I forgot to reply to that email."

Once named, these thoughts immediately lose some power.

The Three-Minute Breathing Space

This one's perfect for busy days:

1. **Minute one:** Notice what's happening in your mind and body right now. No judging, just noticing.

2. **Minute two:** Focus completely on the sensation of breathing.

3. **Minute three:** Expand awareness to your whole body.

I've done this while waiting for coffee, sitting on trains, and even in bathroom stalls during stressful meetings (hey, we do what we must).

The "What's Not Wrong Right Now?" Practice

Our brains are wired to scan for problems. Counter this by asking, "What's actually okay right now?"

Maybe your feet are comfortable. The air is breathable. Your heart is beating without your supervision (thanks, heart!). This isn't toxic positivity, it's reality checking.

The "Feel Your Feet" Reset

Whenever you catch yourself overthinking, immediately shift attention to the sensation of your feet against the floor. Feel the pressure, temperature, and texture. This instantly pulls you back to your body in the present moment.

I keep a sticky note on my laptop that says "FEET!" As strange as it looks to visitors, it's saved me from countless overthinking spirals. Remember, the goal isn't to empty your mind or never think about the past or future.

That's impossible (and sometimes unhelpful). The goal is to recognize when you're no longer present and have a toolkit to bring yourself back.

With practice, you'll start catching yourself earlier in the overthinking cycle. That pause—that moment of noticing—is your growing power of presence. It's the difference between being dragged around by your thoughts and remembering that you're the one who's supposed to be driving this thing.

Mind-Quieting Magic: Simple Practices for Chaotic Brains

You don't need to be a Zen master to find some mental quiet. Let's explore some down-to-earth practices that can help tame that mental circus.

Breathing: Your Built-in Chill Button

Remember when someone told you to "just breathe" during a stressful moment, and you wanted to scream? Turns out, they weren't entirely wrong, just really bad at explaining why.

Try this: Breathe in for a count of four, hold for two, and exhale for six. When we extend our exhale longer than our inhale, we actually trigger our parasympathetic nervous system—the body's "rest and digest" mode.

I've used this during panic-inducing work presentations and while trying to assemble furniture with instructions clearly written by sadists.

The 4-7-8 breath works wonders too: Inhale for 4, hold for 7, and exhale for 8. Just three rounds can noticeably calm an overthinking storm.

The first time I tried this before bed, I was genuinely annoyed at how well it worked; I'd spent years battling insomnia with far more complicated methods.

Mother Nature: The Original Therapist

Forest bathing sounds like something involving outdoor tubs and mosquitoes, but it's actually just mindfully spending time among trees. There's science behind why a walk in natural settings calms us, something about fractal patterns and negative ions that our ancestors evolved with.

You don't need actual forests either. A neighborhood park, a tree-lined street, and even watching leaves move outside your window count. The key is to really notice the different shades of green, the patterns of light, and the sounds of birds or rustling leaves.

My personal overthinking kryptonite is water: oceans, lakes, even streams in city parks. Something about moving water seems to wash away mental noise. One particularly anxious day, I sat by a fountain for twenty minutes and left feeling like I'd had a brain massage.

Body Scan: The Ultimate Reality Check

When thoughts won't stop spinning, try this: Starting at your toes and working upward, mentally scan each part of your body. Notice sensations without judgment: pressure, temperature, tension, and relaxation.

This practice works because you cannot simultaneously focus on physical sensations and spin overthinking narratives. It's like trying to watch two movies at once; the brain simply can't do it. I once caught myself catastrophizing about a minor work issue while doing a body scan.

By the time I reached my shoulders, I realized they were practically touching my ears from tension, over an email! This awareness alone helped me laugh and let go.

Guided Meditations: Mental Training Wheels

If sitting in silence makes your thoughts louder, try guided meditations. Having someone's voice direct your attention gives your thinking mind a job; just follow the instructions. Apps, YouTube, and many libraries offer free options.

Start with just five minutes. I began with three minutes because even five seemed impossible for my squirrel brain.

Now, I can do fifteen without mentally redecorating my house or planning dinner.

The Three-Step Emergency De-Frazzle

When overthinking hits hard:

1. Name five things you can see.

2. Take three deliberate breaths.

3. Press your feet firmly into the floor.

This simple sequence interrupts the thought spiral by forcing your attention into your senses. I call it my "panic pivot" and have used it everywhere from job interviews to first dates.

Remember, these practices aren't about achieving perfect mental silence (does anyone actually get that?). They're about creating space between you and your thoughts—just enough room to remember that you are not your thoughts, and not every thought deserves your full attention.

Reality Check: Finding Peace in What Actually Is

Let's talk about that voice in your head—you know the one. The commentator who's never satisfied, the one who replays embarrassing moments from 2015 at 3 a.m., or spins elaborate disaster scenarios about next week's presentation. If that voice had its own reality show, it would be called "Overanalyzing Everything."

Here's the truth: That voice isn't you. It's just a noisy roommate you never asked for.

Mindfulness offers something radical: the chance to step back and observe that voice without believing everything it says. And in that space between you and your thoughts lies freedom from the overthinking trap.

The Art of Mental Decluttering

Think of your mind like your living space. When it's cluttered with old regrets, future worries, and unnecessary "what-ifs," there's hardly room to exist in the present moment.

I realized this one morning while making coffee. I was physically standing in my kitchen, but mentally I was rehearsing an argument with my boss that hadn't happened (and never did). I had completely missed the smell of the coffee, the warmth of the mug, the morning light—actual, real things happening right then.

Mental decluttering starts with a simple question: "Is this thought about something real and happening right now?" If not, you can acknowledge it and gently set it aside, not forever, just for this moment.

It's like having a messy junk drawer. You don't need to throw everything away; you just need to stop rummaging through it when you're trying to cook dinner.

The Self-Acceptance Paradox

One of mindfulness's greatest gifts is the realization that you don't need to fix yourself to find peace. In fact, the constant fixing attempts—the endless self-improvement projects—often fuel overthinking.

Try this weird paradox: What if you're actually okay exactly as you are right now?

I know, I know. My inner critic screamed when I first encountered this idea. But there's freedom in temporarily putting down the self-improvement project and simply being with yourself as you are.

Next time you catch yourself overthinking, try saying, "Even with these thoughts, I'm okay." Not perfect, not finished growing, just basically okay in this moment.

From Imagination to Reality

Overthinking loves to pull us into elaborate stories. "If I say this, then they'll think that, which will make them do this, and eventually lead to disaster." Sound familiar?

The mindful approach asks, What do I actually know right now? Not what I'm imagining, remembering, or forecasting—what's real?

Last year, I spent three weeks worrying about a medical test result. My mind created vivid scenarios of treatments, telling people how life would change, complete with emotional soundtracks!

When I finally got the (normal) results, I realized I'd lived through an entire illness that never existed. Mindfulness trains us to distinguish between actual facts and the stories we build around them. It's the difference between "My friend hasn't texted back" (fact) and "My friend is mad at me forever because I'm a terrible person" (story).

The Present Moment Scavenger Hunt

Try this game: Throughout your day, collect moments of simple awareness. The taste of your lunch. The feeling of a breeze. The sound of laughter.

These small moments of presence add up, gradually training your mind to stay more often in what's real rather than what's imagined. They're like little weights strengthening your present-moment muscles.

Mindfulness isn't about having an empty mind; it's about having a mind that knows the difference between what's happening and what's being imagined. And in that difference lies freedom from the overthinking trap.

Chapter 7:

Letting Go of Perfection

I once spent three hours writing an email. Not a book chapter, not a business proposal, but a simple email to a colleague. I rewrote the opening line seventeen times. I agonized over word choices as if lives depended on them. I even changed fonts twice, despite knowing the recipient would see it in whatever default email font they used.

Perfectionism might be the most exhausting form of overthinking. It masquerades as high standards and attention to detail, but in reality, it's a relentless inner critic that whispers, "Not good enough yet," when everyone else is saying, "This is great!"

The Never-Ending Search: When Perfect Becomes the Enemy of Done

I once spent two weeks choosing a coffee table. Not because I couldn't find one; I found dozens. But what if the round one looked better than the rectangular one? What if the wooden one scratched easily? What if the glass one would show fingerprints? What if there was a *perfect* coffee table just one more website away?

Meanwhile, my living room remained table-less, with guests balancing drinks on their knees.

The Perfectionist Brain: Always On the Hunt

Perfectionists don't just want good solutions; they want THE solution. The flawless, unimpeachable, everyone-will-be-impressed solution. And therein lies the problem.

While most people can say, "This option looks good enough; let's go with it," the perfectionist thinks, "But what if there's something better I haven't considered yet?" It's like being stuck in a mental revolving door, spinning through the same options again and again, unable to exit.

My friend Lisa, a graphic designer, once confessed she had 37 versions of a client's logo saved on her computer. When I asked which one she submitted, she laughed nervously and said, "I'm still working on it." The deadline was three days earlier.

The Fear Factory: Making Mountains of Molehills

Behind perfectionism lurks something most of us don't want to admit: fear. Fear of criticism. Fear of failure. Fear of not measuring up.

When we believe that making mistakes equals being a failure, we'll do mental gymnastics to avoid any possible error. Every decision becomes not just a choice but a reflection of our worth.

Perfectionism turns molehills into mountains and mountains into Mount Everests. No wonder we overthink; we're trying to climb Everest in flip-flops.

The Impossible Math of Perfection

Here's the math problem perfectionists set for themselves:

- Consider all possible options (infinite).

- Predict all possible outcomes (also infinite).

- Choose the one perfect solution with zero downsides.

No wonder our brains get stuck in loops! We've assigned ourselves a literally impossible task.

Breaking the Loop: First Steps

Understanding this connection is your first step toward freedom. When you catch yourself in an overthinking spiral, ask:

- *Am I searching for perfect, or would good enough actually work here?*

- *What's the real cost of delaying this decision while seeking perfection?*

- *If a friend were in my position, what would I advise them?*

Sometimes, I set a "decision timer" for less important choices. Ten minutes to pick a restaurant. Thirty minutes to choose a gift. When the timer goes off, I go with the best option I've found so far. The world hasn't ended yet.

Loosening the Grip: How to Stop Micromanaging Your Life

My friend Jake once missed his flight because he insisted on reorganizing his entire suitcase at the check-in counter. Everything had to be perfectly folded, categorized, and arranged by color. Meanwhile, the final boarding call echoed through the terminal. When I asked why he didn't just fix it later, he looked genuinely confused. "But it wouldn't be right," he said.

The need to control is perfectionism's bossy older sibling. It's not just about doing things flawlessly; it's about making sure everything and everyone around us meets our exacting standards, too. Let's look at some practical ways to loosen that white-knuckle grip on life without feeling like we're free-falling into chaos.

Practice the Art of Strategic Sloppiness

Yes, you read that right. Try deliberately doing something slightly imperfectly. Leave one dish unwashed. Send an email with a typo. Let your partner load the dishwasher their way.

The first time I tried this, I left a small pile of laundry unfolded overnight. I actually checked on it twice to make sure it wasn't somehow multiplying or causing household disasters. By morning, I had to admit something shocking: absolutely nothing bad happened.

Start with low-stakes situations and work your way up. Think of it as exposure therapy for your inner control freak.

Embrace "Good Enough" as a Legitimate Destination

For control enthusiasts, "good enough" sounds like settling for mediocrity. But here's a perspective shift: Good enough is often the optimal balance between effort and outcome.

Try the 80/20 rule: Recognize that you'll get about 80% of the value from the first 20% of the effort. Those final perfectionist touches? They're usually invisible to everyone but you.

Delegate Without Hovering

The hardest part of delegation isn't assigning tasks—it's resisting the urge to peek over shoulders every thirty seconds. Next time you delegate, try this: Set clear expectations, then physically remove yourself from the situation. Go for a walk. Work in another room. Turn off your phone if you have to. I once asked my partner to plan our weekend trip. For three days, I bit my tongue to avoid asking questions or making suggestions. The result? A fantastic trip I never would have planned, with surprises I couldn't have anticipated. Plus, he felt trusted and appreciated.

Break Down the Mountain

Control issues often flare up when we face complex tasks. Everything feels important when you're staring at one massive challenge.

Try breaking things down into smaller chunks, then ask, "If I had to pick just three essential elements to focus on, what would they be?"

For a presentation, maybe it's the main message, one compelling visual, and answering the obvious questions. For a dinner party, perhaps it's good food, comfortable seating, and a welcoming atmosphere. The rest is just bonus material.

Reality-Check Your Catastrophizing

When the thought of relinquishing control makes you panicky, challenge those thoughts:

- What's the worst that could realistically happen?

- How would I handle that outcome if it did occur?

- What's the cost of maintaining this level of control?

I once refused to let anyone help with Thanksgiving dinner. By the time guests arrived, I was sweaty, cranky, and too exhausted to enjoy the company.

The following year, I let people bring dishes and help with setup. Was everything exactly as I would have done it? No. Was it still a lovely meal with much better company? Absolutely.

Treat Yourself Like a Friend

Notice your self-talk when things aren't perfect. Would you speak to a friend that way? Probably not. Next time you catch yourself saying, "I can't believe I messed that up. I'm so incompetent," try switching to, "Well, that didn't go as planned, but I'll figure it out."

Remember, the goal isn't to abandon all standards. It's to create space for being human—imperfect, sometimes messy, and ultimately much happier when we're not trying to control every molecule in our path.

Thriving in Disaster: Finding Freedom in Flaws

My bathroom wall has a small dent where I once tried to hang a towel rack. I missed the stud, the rack pulled out, and I was left with damaged drywall and wounded pride. For months, that dent bothered me every time I saw it—a glaring reminder of my imperfection.

Then one day, my five-year-old niece pointed at it and asked what happened. After I explained my DIY disaster, she shrugged and said, "Everyone messes up sometimes. My teacher says that's how we get smarter."

Out of the mouths of babes, as they say. Most of us weren't born perfectionists; we learned it somewhere along the way. Which means we can unlearn it, too.

Redefining Mistakes as Plot Twists

What if we viewed mistakes not as failures but as unexpected plot developments in our life story?

When I accidentally added salt instead of sugar to a cake recipe (yes, really), I discovered that salt actually enhances chocolate flavor in small amounts. My "mistake" led me to experiment with salted desserts long before they became trendy.

Next time something goes wrong, try asking, "What does this make possible now?" instead of "How did I mess up?"

This simple shift can transform a dead end into a detour that might lead somewhere interesting.

Building Your Resilience Muscles

Think of making "imperfect" decisions as strength training for your resilience muscles. Each time you survive a less-than-ideal outcome, you prove to yourself that you can handle it.

Start with low-stakes decisions where the consequences don't matter much. Order something unusual at a restaurant. Take a different route home. Wear that bold outfit you're not sure about.

I once showed up to a meeting with mismatched shoes (black and navy in similar styles). Instead of dying from embarrassment, I pointed it out with a laugh.

Not only did everyone forget about it by the next day, but it actually broke the ice in what had been a tense project.

The "Worst-Case Reality Check"

When perfectionism paralyzes you, try this technique:

1. Ask yourself, "What's the absolute worst realistic outcome of this decision?"

2. Then ask, "Could I handle that if it happened?"

3. Finally: "What resources or support would help me handle it?"

I use this when public speaking, which terrifies me. Worst case? I mess up badly and feel embarrassed. Could I handle that? Yes, though it would be uncomfortable. Resources?

Breathing techniques, supportive friends, and the knowledge that everyone forgets about these things quickly.

Suddenly, the fear loses some of its power.

The 70% Rule

Waiting until you're 100% certain is a recipe for paralysis. Instead, try the 70% rule: If you're about 70% confident in a decision, that's usually enough to proceed.

This rule acknowledges that perfect certainty is rare. Even experts make educated guesses. The difference is that they don't let uncertainty stop them from moving forward.

When I was torn between two job offers, I realized I'd never be 100% sure which was best. But I was about 75% confident in one direction, so I made the leap.

Six years later, it remains one of the best decisions I've made.

Building a Mistake-Friendly Environment

Surround yourself with people who don't expect perfection. Share your fears and mishaps with trusted friends. Laugh at yourself when appropriate. Celebrate others who take risks, even when they don't pan out perfectly.

In my house, we now have a monthly "failure dinner" where everyone shares something that didn't go as planned and what they learned. It's become a surprisingly fun tradition that has slowly rewired how we all view mistakes.

The Freedom in "Oh Well"

Perhaps the most powerful phrase in the imperfection toolkit is simply "Oh well."

Sent an email with a typo? Oh well. Said something awkward in a meeting? Oh well. Made the wrong choice at a restaurant? Oh well.

This isn't about not caring or lowering standards. It's about the appropriate emotional response. Not everything deserves the weight we give it.

Remember, embracing imperfection isn't about celebrating mediocrity. It's about freeing yourself from the paralysis of perfectionism so you can actually accomplish more, experience more, and yes, even excel more in the things that truly matter.

Part 3:

Cultivating Balance and Vitality

Chapter 8:

The Art of Decision-Making

Standing in the cereal aisle, I watched a woman hold two boxes of oatmeal for what seemed like twenty minutes. She'd pick up one, read the label, put it back, grab the other, compare prices, check ingredients again, and then start the whole process over. I actually finished my entire grocery shopping, and she was still there when I passed by on my way out.

I recognized that look, the paralyzed expression of someone trapped in decision limbo. I'd worn it myself countless times, from choosing restaurants to picking career paths. It's the face of an overthinker who knows that somewhere out there exists the "perfect choice," and settling for anything less feels like giving up.

From Chaos to Choice: Breaking Down Decisions Into Bite-Sized Pieces

I once stood in front of my closet for thirty minutes trying to decide what to wear to a casual dinner. Thirty minutes! Meanwhile, my friend Tania could plan an entire vacation in the same time. What was her secret? She had learned something I hadn't: good decision-making isn't about being smarter; it's about having a process.

Most of us approach decisions like we're trying to solve a jigsaw puzzle in the dark while someone shouts random instructions. No wonder we get overwhelmed. But when you break decision-making into manageable steps, even complex choices become surprisingly straightforward.

Step 1: Narrow Down the Real Question

Before going into options, get crystal clear on what you're actually deciding. This sounds obvious, but overthinkers often expand simple choices into philosophical dilemmas.

"Should I change jobs?" becomes "What's my life purpose, and how do I achieve career fulfillment while maintaining work-life balance?" when the real question might be "Am I happy enough here to stay another year?"

My neighbor spent months agonizing over whether to renovate her kitchen until she realized she was really asking, "Do I want to live in this house long-term?" Once she answered that (yes), the renovation decision became much simpler.

Step 2: Understand What Really Matters

Not all factors in a decision carry equal weight. Smart decision-makers identify their top three priorities and focus on them.

When I was choosing between apartments, I initially considered seventeen different factors: from ceiling height to proximity to my favorite coffee shop. But when I narrowed it down to my actual priorities (price, commute time, and having enough space for guests), the choice became obvious.

Ask yourself, "If I could only consider three things about this decision, what would they be?"

Step 3: Take It in Small Bites

Complex decisions don't have to be made all at once. Break them into smaller, manageable pieces and tackle them one at a time.

Choosing a career path? Start by exploring what type of work environment you prefer. Deciding where to live? First, narrow down the geographic region, then the neighborhood, then specific properties.

My friend Lisa wanted to start a business but felt overwhelmed by all the decisions involved. We broke it down: first, she'd validate the business idea by talking to potential customers. Only after getting positive feedback would she move to step two: creating a basic business plan. This approach turned a paralyzing choice into a series of small, doable steps.

Step 4: Set Your Research Limits

Here's where overthinkers get stuck: endless information gathering. Productive decision-makers set boundaries on their research phase.

Try the "three sources rule"; for most decisions, three good sources of information are enough. More than that and you're probably procrastinating rather than researching.

When buying my car, I gave myself one week to research and two dealerships to visit. Without those limits, I would have researched until the car industry evolved to flying vehicles.

Step 5: Listen to Input (But Don't Crowdsource)

Good decision-makers seek relevant input without turning every choice into a democracy. Ask one or two people whose judgment you trust, not your entire social network.

I learned this the hard way when I asked everyone for restaurant recommendations for a first date. I received fourteen different suggestions and spent so much time weighing options that I was twenty minutes late to dinner.

Step 6: Recognize "Good Enough" When You See It

Perfect decisions are rare. Good ones are everywhere. When you find an option that meets your main criteria and doesn't have any deal-breaking flaws, that's often your answer.

The apartment that checks your three priority boxes? Take it. The job that offers growth in your field and reasonable pay? Say yes. The restaurant with good reviews and a convenient location? Make the reservation.

The Magic of Time Limits

Perhaps the most important skill is setting decision deadlines. Without them, choices expand to fill infinite time.

For small decisions (what to order, which movie to watch), give yourself two minutes. Medium decisions (which phone to buy, vacation destination) get a day or two.

Big decisions (job changes, major purchases) might deserve a week or a month, but not more.

The goal isn't to make perfect decisions; it's to make good decisions and move forward with confidence. The best choice is often the one that gets you unstuck and moving toward your goals, even if it's not theoretically optimal.

Decision-making is a skill, and like any skill, it improves with practice. Start with small, low-stakes choices and work your way up.

Before long, you'll find yourself spending less time agonizing and more time living.

Your Decision-Making Toolkit: Fast and Confident Choices

My uncle Jim can walk into any restaurant and order within thirty seconds. I used to think he was just indecisive or didn't care about food quality. Turns out, he had a system: scan the menu for three things that sound good, pick the first one that fits his budget, done. While I spent fifteen minutes agonizing over every option, he was already enjoying his meal.

That's when I realized successful decision-makers aren't necessarily smarter; they just have better tools.

The 80/20 Rule: Your New Best Friend

This rule states that 80% of your results come from 20% of your efforts. In decision-making terms, you'll get 80% of the benefit from the first 20% of information you gather.

When I was house-hunting, I initially planned to research every neighborhood, school district, and future development plan in the city. My realtor (a wise woman) suggested I focus on three neighborhoods that met my basic needs. Within those areas, I found my perfect home in two weeks instead of the six months I'd planned.

The lesson? Get enough information to make a good decision, then stop researching and start deciding.

Smart Education vs. Information Overload

There's a difference between educating yourself and drowning in data. Smart education means understanding the basics well enough to spot good options and avoid obvious mistakes.

For most decisions, you need to know:

- What are the main factors that matter?

- What's a reasonable price range or timeline?

- What are the major red flags to avoid?

When I bought my first car, I spent one evening learning about reliability ratings, typical price ranges, and what to look for during a test drive. That basic knowledge was enough to make a good choice without becoming an automotive expert.

Trusting Your Gut (Yes, Really)

Your intuition isn't mystical; it's your brain processing patterns and information faster than your conscious mind can track. That "gut feeling" often contains valuable data.

Try this: after gathering basic information about a decision, sit quietly for a moment and notice your first instinct. Not the voice analyzing pros and cons, but the immediate feeling of "yes" or "no" in your body.

I used to dismiss gut feelings as unscientific until I started tracking them. Turns out, my initial instincts were right about 80% of the time. The times I ignored them and chose the "logical" option often led to regret.

Understanding Probability (Without Math Nightmares)

You don't need to be a statistician, but understanding basic probability helps prevent overthinking worst-case scenarios. Ask yourself, "What's the realistic likelihood of this bad outcome?" Often, we treat low-probability events like certainties. Yes, the restaurant might give you food poisoning, but millions of people eat out safely every day. My friend Shasha avoided flying for years because of crash statistics she'd googled. When we looked at actual probability (you're more likely to be struck by lightning), she realized her fear was based on possibility, not probability.

Setting Quick Decision Boundaries

Boundaries prevent endless deliberation. Before you start researching any decision, set limits:

- How much time will I spend on this?

- How much information is enough?

- What's my budget or other hard constraints?

For minor decisions, I use the "two-minute rule": If it won't matter in two years, spend at most two minutes deciding. For bigger choices, I might allocate a weekend or a week, but never more.

The "Good Enough" Filter

Most decisions don't require optimization; they require action. Train yourself to recognize when an option meets your main criteria and has no deal-breaking flaws.

That apartment with a good location and reasonable rent? Take it, even if the kitchen isn't your dream setup. The job that offers growth and decent pay? Accept it, even if the office coffee is terrible.

Perfect is the enemy of good, and good is usually good enough to move your life forward. Most "wrong" decisions teach us something valuable and can be corrected along the way.

You're Better at This Than You Think: Building Trust in Your Own Judgment

My friend Rachel once called me at midnight, panicked about a job decision she'd been weighing for weeks. She'd researched the company, talked to current employees, and created a detailed pros-and-cons list. Yet she was terrified of making the wrong choice.

"What does your gut say?" I asked.

"That it's a good opportunity," she admitted. "But what if I'm wrong?"

"What if you're right?" I countered.

That simple question changed everything. Rachel had done her homework. She had good instincts. But somewhere along the way, she'd forgotten to trust herself.

Your Hidden Track Record

Stop for a moment and think about all the decisions you've made that worked out well. You chose friends who enriched your life. You learned skills that served you. You navigated challenges and came out stronger.

Sure, you've made some choices you'd do differently. We all have. But overthinking often makes us forget our successes while magnifying our mistakes.

I keep a "wins journal" where I write down good decisions I've made, big and small. Choosing to learn a new software program helped my career. Deciding to attend that networking event, where I met great friends. Even small wins, like picking the perfect restaurant for a special dinner.

Reading through it reminds me that my judgment is actually pretty solid most of the time.

The Preparation-Confidence Connection

Here's the secret successful decision-makers know: Confidence comes from preparation, not perfection.

When you've done reasonable research, considered your priorities, and thought through the basics, you're equipped to make a good choice. Not a perfect choice, but a good one.

Before my last job interview, I spent an evening researching the company, practicing common questions, and thinking about how my experience aligned with their needs. Walking into that interview, I felt prepared and confident. Did I answer every question perfectly? No. But I trusted that my preparation was enough.

Your Instincts Are Smarter Than You Think

That gut feeling isn't random; it's your brain processing information rapidly based on patterns and experiences you might not consciously remember.

When something feels "off" about a situation, that's often your subconscious picking up on subtle cues. When something feels "right," that's your brain recognizing positive patterns from your past experience.

I learned to trust this during apartment hunting. On paper, one place checked all my boxes. But something felt wrong during the visit. I couldn't pinpoint why, so I almost ignored it. Fortunately, I trusted the feeling and kept looking. Later, I discovered the neighborhood had serious parking issues that weren't immediately obvious, exactly the kind of detail my subconscious had somehow detected.

The Mistake: Fear Reality Check

Fear of making mistakes often stems from catastrophic thinking. We imagine that one wrong choice will derail our entire life. But think about it: How many of your past "mistakes" actually led to disaster?

Most poor decisions are reversible or teachable. The job that didn't work out led to better opportunities. The relationship that ended taught valuable lessons. The purchase you regretted became a funny story.

Very few decisions are truly irreversible. Most can be adjusted, learned from, or completely changed if needed.

Building Your Confidence Muscle

Like any skill, trusting your judgment gets stronger with practice. Start with small, low-stakes decisions and work your way up.

Choose a restaurant without reading every review. Pick a movie based on your initial interest. Buy the shirt you like without asking three friends for opinions. Each time you make a decision and survive the outcome (good or bad), you prove to yourself that you can handle the consequences of your choices.

The Permission to Be Human

Perhaps most importantly, give yourself permission to make imperfect decisions. You're not a computer calculating optimal outcomes; you're a human being navigating a complex world with incomplete information. Remember Rachel? She took that job. Six months later, she told me it was one of the best decisions she'd ever made.

Not because it was perfect, but because she'd trusted herself enough to try. You have good instincts. You've proven it before. Trust them again.

Chapter 9:

The Power of Boundaries

Picture this: You're at a party, and there's that one person who just won't stop talking. They corner you by the snack table and launch into a forty-five-minute monologue about their cousin's pet iguana. You smile politely and nod at the right moments, but inside you're screaming. You know you should excuse yourself, but somehow you just... don't.

Now, imagine your brain doing the exact same thing to you every single day.

When we hear about setting boundaries, we usually think about other people. We learn to say no to extra work projects, to pushy relatives, or to friends who always need a favor. And yes, that stuff matters. But here's what catches most of us off guard: It's also necessary to set boundaries with yourself.

When Your Brain Needs a Vacation (But You Can't Give It One)

Ever feel like your head is stuffed with cotton balls and your emotions are doing the cha-cha? Welcome to mental and emotional overload—that special kind of exhaustion where even deciding what to have for lunch feels like solving calculus.

Here's the thing: Boundaries reduce mental and emotional overload, whether you establish them between yourself and others or limit yourself in certain thoughts or behaviors. Think of boundaries as your personal air traffic controller, deciding what gets to land in your mental airport and what needs to circle around until further notice. Let's start with the obvious stuff—boundaries with other people. You know that friend who texts you their entire life story at 11 p.m.? Or your coworker who dumps their stress on you every Monday morning like you're their personal therapist? Without boundaries, you're basically running a 24-hour emotional support hotline. And frankly, most of us didn't sign up for that job.

When you don't have these boundaries, your brain becomes a dumping ground for everyone else's problems on top of your own. It's like trying to juggle flaming torches while someone keeps tossing you more. Eventually, something's going to get burned, and it's probably going to be you.

But here's where it gets tricky. The boundaries you need most are often the ones with yourself. Your mind loves to replay conversations from three years ago or create detailed disaster movies about things that will probably never happen. Without internal boundaries, you're letting your brain run wild like a toddler with a sugar rush in a toy store.

I used to think that entertaining every worried thought made me "thorough" or "prepared." Turns out, I was just wearing myself out. It's like doing mental jumping jacks all day—you get tired, but you don't actually get anywhere.

When you set boundaries with your thoughts, you're not ignoring problems or being irresponsible. You're choosing which thoughts deserve your time and energy. Some thoughts are worth your attention, like remembering to pay bills or planning your weekend. Others are just mental junk mail that somehow got past your spam filter.

The magic happens when you start treating your mental space like your physical space. You wouldn't let strangers walk into your house and rearrange your furniture, so why let random thoughts waltz into your head and redecorate your mood? Boundaries aren't walls—they're more like smart filters that help you focus on what actually matters.

Your Personal Boundary Blueprint

Setting boundaries sounds great in theory, but where do you actually put them? It's not like you can just buy a "Boundary Kit" on Amazon (though honestly, wouldn't that make life easier?). The truth is, you need boundaries in two main areas: outside your head and inside it.

The External Stuff (AKA Other People's Drama)

Let's start with the obvious culprits. Your relationships need boundaries; yes, even the good ones. That friend who calls during your favorite show, expecting a two-hour therapy session? Boundary needed. Your coworker who thinks "urgent" means "I just thought of this?"

Another boundary candidate.

Work boundaries are huge. If you're answering emails at midnight or taking calls during dinner, you've basically invited your job to move in rent-free. Your boss might not love it at first, but even they don't want a burned-out zombie on their team.

Then there's family: The people who knew you when you had braces and still think they can tell you how to live. Whether it's your spouse expecting you to read their mind or your mom still treating you like you're twelve, family boundaries can feel scary, but they're often the most important ones. Don't forget self-care boundaries either. Yes, saying no to that third commitment this week counts as self-care.

So does not checking your phone first thing in the morning or actually taking your lunch break instead of eating a sad sandwich at your desk.

The Internal Battlefield (AKA Your Own Personal Soap Opera)

Here's where things get interesting. You also need boundaries with your own thoughts and memories. Past experiences love to crash your present-day party uninvited. That embarrassing thing from high school? It doesn't get to ruin your Tuesday afternoon twenty years later.

Trauma has a way of barging into random moments, and family dysfunction can echo in your head long after you've moved out. These need boundaries too; not because you're ignoring what happened, but because you're choosing when and how to deal with it.

Poor self-image and negative self-talk are like having a mean roommate in your brain who never pays rent but always has opinions. You wouldn't let someone else talk to you the way you sometimes talk to yourself, so why give your inner critic a free pass?

And overthinking? That's the big one. Your brain will happily chew on problems all day if you let it. Sometimes you need to tell your thoughts, "Thanks for sharing, but we're closed for business right now."

The Art of No: A Masterclass in Not Being Everyone's Yes-Person

Let's talk about the hardest two-letter word in the English language: no. It's shorter than "hi" and simpler than "um," yet somehow saying it feels harder than explaining quantum physics to a goldfish.

The External No: Why You're Not a Human Vending Machine

Here's the thing about saying no without guilt: You have to stop treating yourself like you're a 24-hour convenience store. You know, always open, always stocked, and somehow expected to have exactly what everyone needs at any hour.

The guilt hits because we've been conditioned to think that saying no makes us selfish. But here's a reality check: If you say yes to everything, you're essentially saying no to yourself. And last time I checked, you matter too.

Start small. That PTA meeting you don't have time for? "Sorry, I can't make it." That extra project when you're already drowning? "I'm at capacity right now." Notice how you don't need a dissertation-length explanation. "No" is a complete sentence, even if it feels weird at first.

The secret sauce is prioritizing what truly matters. Make a list of your top three priorities right now. Got it? Good. Now, when someone asks you to do something, check if it fits those three things. If it doesn't, you have your answer.

Don't overburden yourself by accepting every offer or opportunity that comes your way. I used to think every opportunity was a gift I couldn't refuse.

Turns out, some gifts are just really pretty boxes full of stress and sleepless nights. Not every door you could walk through is worth walking through.

The Internal No: Setting Boundaries With Your Own Brain

Now, here's where it gets interesting: You also need to say no to yourself. Your brain is like that friend who means well but gives terrible advice at 2 a.m. Sometimes you just have to cut the conversation short.

As a step toward stopping the overthinking habit, only allow yourself to ruminate for a limited amount of time. Set a timer if you have to. "Okay, brain, you get fifteen minutes to worry about this thing, and then we're moving on." It sounds ridiculous, but it works better than letting your thoughts run marathons in your head all day.

Some wounds need professional help. If you're carrying around emotional baggage that's affecting your daily life, seek counseling. There's no shame in getting a professional to help you sort through the mess. Think of it like calling a plumber when your sink won't stop leaking; some problems need expert hands.

Here's a weird thought: treat yourself like you would a good friend. If your friend was constantly putting themselves down, you'd tell them to knock it off, right? Do the same with your internal self-talk. Don't accept certain attitudes or harsh words from your inner voice that you wouldn't accept from anyone else.

Practice gratitude to combat overthinking. When your brain starts its doom-and-gloom playlist, interrupt it with three things you're grateful for. It's like changing the radio station from heavy metal to something that doesn't give you a headache. Pay attention to what situations you place yourself in and what people you allow into your life. Some people are overthinking triggers while walking around in human form. You know the type; they turn "beautiful day" into "But what if it rains tomorrow and ruins everything?" If you can't avoid them completely, at least limit your exposure.

Dealing With Other People's Overthinking

Speaking of overthinking triggers, let's talk about dealing with others who are overthinkers. You can't fix them (trust me, I've tried), but you can set boundaries. When they start spiraling, you can say, "I can see you're really worried about this. Have you thought about talking to someone who can actually help?" Then redirect the conversation or excuse yourself.

You're not their therapist, and you're not required to get sucked into their mental whirlpool just because they're drowning in it.

Making Peace With Your Past

Establish boundaries with your past, too. You can't change what's already happened; I know, shocking revelation. It's futile to continue dwelling on things you can't fix. Your past already happened, and no amount of mental replay is going to change the ending.

This doesn't mean pretending bad things didn't happen. It means saying, "That was then, this is now, and I'm not going to let yesterday hijack today." Give your past a time limit, too. "I'll think about this for ten minutes, learn what I can from it, and then I'm focusing on what I can actually control."

Setting boundaries isn't about becoming mean or selfish. It's about becoming the person who gets to decide how their time and energy get spent. And honestly? That person deserves to be you.

Chapter 10:

Building Resilience Against Stress

Here's some good news that might surprise you: Overthinking is not a disease, and it's not a mental disorder. It's a habit, and as such, it can be stopped. You can learn from the experience and build up your resilience to strengthen your character as you move ahead.

I know what you're thinking: "If it's just a habit, why does it feel so impossible to break?" Fair question. But think about it this way: Biting your nails is also just a habit, yet plenty of people struggle with it for years.

The difference between overthinking and nail-biting is that overthinking happens inside your head, where nobody can see it, so it feels more mysterious and permanent than it actually is.

The truth is, you've probably already broken dozens of habits in your lifetime without even thinking about it. Remember when you used to check Facebook every five minutes? Or when you couldn't go to sleep without watching TV? Most habits fade away so gradually that we don't even notice we've stopped doing them.

Overthinking feels different because it seems to serve a purpose. Your brain tricks you into believing that all that mental spinning is actually productive, like you're problem-solving or preparing for the worst. But here's the reality check:

There's a huge difference between thinking something through and thinking something to death.

Your Anti-Overthinking Toolkit (Some Assembly Required)

Think of stress management techniques like having a good toolbox. You don't need every tool ever invented, but you want a few reliable ones that actually work when your mental pipes start leaking or your emotional circuit breaker trips.

The Greatest Hits (AKA What We've Already Covered)

Let's do a quick recap of some tools we've already put in your toolkit. Mindfulness is still your MVP—that simple practice of noticing what's happening right now instead of spiraling into what-if land. It's like having a mental anchor that keeps you from drifting into overthinking territory.

CBT techniques are your logic squad. When your brain starts creating disaster movies, CBT helps you fact-check the script. "Is this thought helpful? Is it even true? What would I tell a friend dealing with this?" Sometimes your brain needs a good reality check, and CBT is great at providing one.

Moving Your Body (Because Your Brain Lives There Too)

Here's something that took me way too long to figure out: Your body and mind aren't separate entities having a polite conversation. They're more like roommates who share everything, including stress. When your mind is spinning, your body feels it. When your body is tense, your mind gets the memo.

Exercise is like hitting the reset button on your stress levels. It doesn't have to be some intense gym session where you look like you're training for the Olympics. A twenty-minute walk works wonders. Dancing in your living room counts too, and yes, I'm talking about the kind where you pretend you're in a music video when nobody's watching.

The beauty of movement is that it gives your overthinking brain something else to focus on. Try having an elaborate worry session while you're concentrating on not tripping over your own feet in a dance class. It's surprisingly difficult.

Calming Your Nervous System (The Technical Stuff Made Simple)

Your nervous system is like your body's alarm system, and overthinking keeps hitting the panic button. Nervous system regulation sounds fancy, but it's really just teaching your body how to chill out.

Yoga and Pilates are fantastic for this. They combine movement with breathing, which is like giving your nervous system a nice cup of chamomile tea. Plus, it's hard to catastrophize about tomorrow's meeting when you're trying to figure out how to balance on one foot without falling over.

Deep breathing exercises work too. I know, I know—"just breathe" sounds like the most useless advice ever when you're stressed. But there's actual science behind it. Slow, deep breaths tell your nervous system, "Hey, we're not being chased by a bear right now. We can relax."

The Fun Stuff (Because Life Shouldn't Be All Work)

Music is pure magic for an overthinking brain. It's like giving your mind permission to focus on something beautiful instead of something stressful. Whether you're listening to it, playing it, or singing off-key in your car, music shifts your mental channel from the worry station to something more pleasant. Hobbies are your secret weapon against overthinking. When you're totally absorbed in gardening, cooking, or building model airplanes, your brain can't multitask its way into a worry spiral. You're present, focused, and giving your overthinking mind a well-deserved break.

The key is finding what works for you. Maybe yoga makes you feel zen, or maybe it makes you feel like a pretzel. That's fine; try dancing instead. Maybe meditation feels impossible, but painting helps you focus. Go with what feels good, not what you think you should do.

The goal isn't to become stress-proof—that's not realistic. The goal is to have reliable ways to dial down the stress when it shows up so it doesn't turn into a full-blown overthinking marathon.

The Body-Brain Connection: Why Your Mental Health Starts with Your Physical Health

Here's something that sounds obvious but somehow gets ignored all the time: Your brain lives in your body. I know, groundbreaking stuff, right? But seriously, we treat our minds like they're floating around in some separate dimension, completely disconnected from whether we've slept, eaten, or moved our bodies in the last 24 hours.

The truth is, how the techniques we've talked about work together with physical activity, nutrition, and sleep contributes to healthy mental energy management and reduces the likelihood of overthinking. Think of it like this: your brain is basically a really demanding houseguest who needs the right environment to behave properly.

Moving Your Body to Quiet Your Mind

Physical activity is like a magic reset button for mental energy. When you're stuck in an overthinking loop, your brain is essentially running in circles like a hamster on a wheel. Exercise gives all that spinning energy somewhere useful to go.

I used to think I was too busy to work out, especially when my mind was racing about deadlines and problems. Turns out, that's exactly when I needed to move the most. A good workout doesn't just tire out your body; it literally changes your brain chemistry. Those feel-good chemicals that get released? They're like nature's chill pills.

You don't need to become a gym rat or train for a marathon. Even a fifteen-minute walk can shift your mental state from "everything is terrible" to "okay, maybe I can handle this." The key is doing something that gets your heart pumping and gives your mind a break from its favorite hobby of worrying about stuff.

Feeding Your Brain (Not Just Your Cravings)

Let's talk about nutrition, and no, I'm not about to tell you to survive on kale smoothies and quinoa. But here's the thing—what you eat directly affects how well your brain works. When you're running on sugar crashes and caffeine spikes, your mental energy is all over the place.

Ever notice how you're more likely to overthink when you're hungry? Or how that 3 p.m. sugar crash makes everything seem more dramatic than it actually is? Your brain needs steady fuel to stay focused and calm. When your blood sugar is doing the roller coaster thing, your thoughts follow right along for the ride. I'm not saying you need to eat perfectly all the time; I still stress-eat cookies when life gets overwhelming. But having some basic protein and eating regular meals instead of surviving on snacks and caffeine makes a huge difference in how much mental energy you have for actual thinking versus spinning your wheels.

Sleep: Your Brain's Maintenance Mode

And then there's sleep: The thing we all know we need more of but somehow always sacrifice first when life gets busy.

Here's what happens when you don't get enough sleep: Your brain basically becomes that friend who's had too much coffee and not enough food. Everything seems like a bigger deal than it is.

Sleep is when your brain does its housekeeping, sorting through the day's information, filing away what's important, and taking out the mental trash. When you're sleep-deprived, all that mental clutter just piles up, making it way easier to get stuck in overthinking mode.

Good sleep doesn't just happen by accident, especially if you're prone to overthinking. Your racing mind loves to throw you a replay of every awkward conversation from the last decade right when your head hits the pillow. Having a wind-down routine, whether it's reading, stretching, or just putting your phone in another room, helps signal to your brain that it's time to stop processing and start resting.

Magic Happens When It All Works Together

The real magic happens when you get all three working together. Regular movement, decent nutrition, and enough sleep create the foundation for mental clarity. When your physical needs are met, your brain has the energy to focus on what actually matters instead of getting hijacked by every random worry that pops up.

It's not about being perfect; it's about giving your brain the basic support it needs to function well.

The Boring Stuff That Actually Works (Sorry, It's Not All Face Masks and Wine)

Let's clear something up right away: When I talk about self-care, I'm not talking about the Instagram version with bubble baths and shopping sprees. Real self-care is way more boring than that, and honestly, that's why it actually works. It's the daily stuff that keeps your mental foundation solid so you don't crumble every time life gets stressful.

Self-Care That Actually Matters

Real self-care starts with the basics, and I mean the really basic stuff. Good hygiene isn't just about not offending people; it's about feeling human. When you're in an overthinking spiral, sometimes a hot shower is the reset button you didn't know you needed. It's hard to catastrophize about tomorrow's presentation when you're focused on how good the hot water feels.

Taking time to do things you enjoy sounds simple, but most overthinkers are terrible at this. We feel guilty for "wasting time" on hobbies or activities that don't have some obvious productivity payoff. But here's the thing: Doing stuff you actually enjoy isn't selfish; it's maintenance. It's like changing the oil in your car. Skip it too long, and eventually something important breaks down.

Dedicating time each day or week to spending time alone isn't about becoming a hermit. It's about giving your brain some quiet space to just be, without having to perform or respond to other people's needs. Even fifteen minutes of sitting with your coffee before everyone else wakes up counts. Your mind needs downtime the same way your phone needs to charge.

The Healthy Habits Nobody Talks About

A balanced diet doesn't mean you have to eat like a fitness influencer. It just means not living off energy drinks and whatever's left in your fridge at midnight. When your blood sugar is stable, your mood is more stable. When your mood is stable, your thoughts are less likely to go off the rails.

I learned this the hard way after spending way too many afternoons convinced everything was falling apart, only to realize I'd forgotten to eat lunch. Turns out, half my "life crises" were actually just low blood sugar tantrums. Who knew?

Getting sunshine and fresh air sounds like advice from your grandmother, but she was onto something. Natural light helps regulate your sleep cycle, and fresh air gives your brain oxygen to think clearly. Plus, being outside for even a few minutes can interrupt a mental spiral just by changing your environment.

The Medical Stuff We Love to Ignore

Here's where it gets really unglamorous: regular medical checkups and staying on top of necessary treatments. I know, I know. Nobody likes going to the doctor or dealing with health stuff when they're busy worrying about everything else. But physical health problems have a sneaky way of making mental health problems worse.

That untreated thyroid issue? It could be making your anxiety worse. Those headaches you keep ignoring? They might be affecting your ability to think clearly. That prescription you stopped taking because you felt better?

Yeah, you probably felt better because the prescription was working. Taking care of your physical health isn't separate from taking care of your mental health; they're the same thing, wearing different outfits.

Why This Boring Stuff Builds Resilience

When you tend to these basic needs consistently, you're building a foundation that can handle stress without cracking. Think of it like this: If your basic needs are met and your body is functioning well, you have way more mental energy available for dealing with actual problems instead of being constantly drained by the basics.

Resilience isn't about being tough enough to handle anything. It's about having enough resources—physical, mental, and emotional—to bounce back when things get hard. And those resources come from the daily, boring habits that nobody posts about on social media.

The beauty of focusing on these fundamentals is that they work even when you don't feel like they're working. You might not notice the difference day to day, but over time, you'll realize you're handling stress better, sleeping more soundly, and spending less time trapped in overthinking loops.

It's not sexy, but it works. And sometimes that's exactly what you need.

Chapter 11:

Cultivating Calm and Inner Peace

Ten chapters into this book, you've probably gotten better at catching yourself when you start spinning out. Maybe you've tried some of the techniques to interrupt those thought loops. That's awesome. But there's still a gap between "not actively freaking out" and actually feeling peaceful, right?

I'm always fascinated by those rare humans who genuinely don't overthink things. They just... exist? Without second-guessing every email they send? Without replaying conversations from 2017? How?

Look, inner peace isn't reserved for meditation gurus or that irritatingly calm friend who does hot yoga and says things like "everything happens for a reason." Even your overthinking brain deserves some quiet time.

The Overthinking Toolkit: Real-World Calm for Your Chaotic Brain

Let's be real—the phrase "practice mindfulness" can trigger an eye-roll so hard you might pull a muscle. Especially when your brain is busy calculating 37 different ways your presentation could go wrong tomorrow while simultaneously replaying that awkward thing you said to your neighbor in 2018.

But here's the thing about finding calm when you're an overthinker: It's less about achieving some mystical state of enlightenment and more about giving your poor, overworked brain something else to do for five freaking minutes.

So, let's talk about what actually works in the real world when your thoughts are bouncing around like a toddler who found the Halloween candy stash.

Get Outside, for Crying Out Loud!

My therapist once told me to "try a nature walk" when I was mid-anxiety spiral. I wanted to throw something at her. But annoyingly, she was right. There's something about feeling grass under your feet or watching leaves do their leaf thing that pulls you out of your head. Even a quick lap around your office building can reset your brain. The overthinking part of your brain hates being reminded that an entire world exists outside your problems.

The Breath Thing Actually Works (I Was Skeptical, Too)

You know how people are always saying "just breathe"?

And you're thinking, "I AM breathing, Karen; that's not the issue here!" But there's a difference between the shallow chest-breathing we do while stress-scrolling Twitter and actual, intentional breathing. Try this: Breathe in for four counts, hold for seven, and exhale for eight. Do it three times when you're spiraling. I was shocked at how quickly it can interrupt a thought tornado.

Yoga: Not Just for Instagram Influencers

I avoided yoga for years because I'm about as flexible as a brick. But it turns out yoga isn't actually about touching your toes or looking cute in expensive leggings. It's about connecting your busy mind to your neglected body. Even five minutes of stretching while focusing on how your muscles feel can snap you out of an overthinking episode. YouTube has tons of "yoga for beginners who can't touch their toes and don't own crystals" videos. Trust me on this one.

Visualization (That Doesn't Require Artistic Talent)

When someone first told me to "visualize my happy place," I genuinely couldn't think of anything except my bed with Netflix and snacks. Which, valid! But visualization can be as simple as imagining your thoughts as leaves floating down a stream; you see them, but you don't jump in after them.

Or picturing your anxiety as a pushy salesperson that you can politely but firmly say "no thanks" to.

The Comfort Stuff That Isn't Meditation

Not everyone finds peace in silence. Sometimes the best way to calm an overthinking brain is to give it just enough distraction:

- Turn on music that matches the mood you want, not the mood you have.

- Surround yourself with soft colors and textures (I literally keep a piece of velvet in my desk drawer to touch when I'm stressed—weird but effective).

- Eat something that reminds you of feeling safe (my go-to overthinking snack is cinnamon toast; it's like a hug for your mouth).

- Pet an animal if you have one (my cat has unwittingly provided thousands of dollars' worth of therapy).

- Rock in a chair or swing in a hammock (the rhythmic motion tells your nervous system, "We're safe now.")

The "I'm Still Overthinking, But at Least I'm Doing Something Else, Too" Activities

Sometimes you can't stop the thoughts, but you can put them in the passenger seat instead of letting them drive.

- Journal it out (even if you just write "this sucks" fifty times).

- Call that friend who gets it (you know the one).

- Sleep with a stuffed animal (no judgment; my stuffed sloth Pablo sees all my 3 a.m. crises).

- Get a fidget toy (they're not just for kids; my spinner has survived many work meetings).

You don't have to be good at any of these things. You just have to try them when your brain is being a jerk. The goal isn't perfect peace; it's just to turn down the volume on your thoughts from "heavy metal concert" to "loud café." And sometimes, that's enough.

Boring Is Beautiful: Why Predictable Routines Save Your Sanity

The word "routine" has a PR problem. It sounds dull, restrictive, and vaguely adult, like fiber supplements or organizing your tax receipts. But for those of us with brains that treat every minor decision as a life-altering crisis, routines aren't boring; they're freaking lifesavers.

Here's something nobody tells you about overthinking: It feeds on uncertainty like a teenager feeds on pizza rolls. Every unstructured moment is an invitation for your brain to helpfully generate 47 different scenarios about what might happen next. Gee, thanks, brain! This is where daily routines come in, not as rigid prison schedules, but as little islands of certainty in your day where your brain can actually take a break from being... well, your brain.

Morning Routines: The Original Reset Button

I'm not going to sit here and tell you to wake up at 5 a.m. to journal and do sun salutations while drinking green juice. If that's your thing, awesome. But for the rest of us mere mortals, a morning routine can be much simpler.

The magic isn't in WHAT you do, but in the blessed predictability of doing it. When you wake up at roughly the same time and follow the same few steps, whether that's "bathroom, coffee, shower, breakfast, teeth" or some other sequence, your brain starts to recognize the pattern. And patterns don't require decisions. And fewer decisions mean less material for your overthinking machine to work with.

My own morning routine isn't Instagram-worthy. It's literally alarm, stare at the ceiling contemplating existence for exactly two minutes, bathroom, coffee (while checking phone despite knowing better), shower, clothes, and breakfast if there's time. But it's my routine, and my anxiety knows the choreography by heart.

Evening Wind-Down: Teaching Your Brain to Shut Up

Your brain is like a toddler at bedtime; it will use ANY excuse to stay up and keep the party going. "But wait! Have we thought about that work email from three weeks ago?

What if it was secretly passive-aggressive? Let's analyze it word by word at 11:43 p.m.!" A consistent bedtime routine is like a lullaby for your overactive mind. It signals, "We're done thinking for today. Thanks for your service. Please clock out now."

The sleep expert I know recommends turning off screens 30 minutes before bed, which always makes me laugh because what am I supposed to do with myself for 30 minutes? Just sit there with my thoughts? The very thoughts I'm trying to escape? Hard pass.

But I've found my own version that works: I still use my phone, but I switch to reading an extremely boring novel instead of scrolling through rage-inducing news. Then, I do the bathroom stuff, put on the same sleep shirt I've had since college (judge away), and make chamomile tea that I'll forget to drink until it's cold.

Is it perfect? No. Does my brain know this sequence means "shut up soon?" Mostly yes.

The Secret Sauce: Consistency, Not Perfection

Here's the thing about routines: They work because you do them most of the time, not because you do them perfectly every time. Your brain doesn't need military precision; it just needs enough familiarity to feel safe.

Some days you'll oversleep. Some nights you'll fall asleep on the couch watching videos of people cleaning their dishwashers (just me?). That's fine. The goal isn't perfection; it's reducing the total number of decisions your poor, overtaxed brain needs to make. Start small. Pick one part of your day that usually feels chaotic, and create even a three-step routine around it. Morning, evening, lunchtime, whatever.

Your overthinking brain will fight it at first, "But what if we need flexibility?" it'll argue, always looking for escape hatches to worry through.

Remind it gently that routines aren't cages; they're hammocks. They hold you when you're too tired to hold yourself. And for overthinkers, that's not boring, it's beautiful.

Mental Jiu-Jitsu: Throwing Your Thoughts Without Getting Thrown

Remember when we were kids and thought quicksand would be a much bigger problem in adult life? Turns out the real quicksand is our own thinking. One negative thought leads to another, and suddenly you're neck-deep in "everyone hates me, and I'll die alone with seventeen cats who will eat my face when I'm gone."

The good news? You can learn to spot the quicksand before you're in too deep. The better news? Even when life truly is a Category 5 hurricane of chaos, you can find that weird calm spot in the middle, like those freaky storm chasers who drive into tornadoes for fun, except without the near-death experience and with more pajamas.

Spotting the Thought Traps (Again)

If you've been skipping around in this book (no judgment, I do the same thing), you might want to flip back to Chapter 4, where we dove deep into thought patterns. But here's the CliffsNotes version for my fellow impatient readers:

Your brain is constantly narrating your life, but it's not exactly Morgan Freeman quality. It's more like that drunk guy at a sports bar who's never actually played the game but has *very* strong opinions about how everyone else is doing it wrong. The first step is simply noticing when this obnoxious announcer starts spouting nonsense. "Oh, there goes my brain again, telling me

I'm going to get fired because my boss didn't use an exclamation point in their email." Just labeling it as a thought, not a fact, creates some breathing room.

The RAIN Method (Not a Weather Forecast)

When you're really stuck in mental quicksand, try this four-step process that some smart people at Forbes came up with (and I've personally tested during countless 3 a.m. panic sessions):

- **R = Recognize:** "Well, hello there, intrusive thought about how everyone at the party secretly hated me! Fancy seeing you again!"

- **A = Accept:** This doesn't mean agreeing with the thought. It just means not fighting it or shoving it down with a mental pillow while it kicks and screams. "Yep, that's definitely a thought I'm having right now. It exists."

- **I = Investigate:** Get curious instead of furious. "Hmm, why might my brain be serving up this particular flavor of anxiety today? Am I tired? Hungry? Did someone tag me in a weird Facebook memory from 2012?"

- **N = Non-identify:** This is the magic part. "This thought is happening, but it's not ME. It's just a thought my brain produced, like how my nose produces snot sometimes. Gross but temporary."

I once used this while convinced a typo in a work email had ended my entire career. By the time I got to the "N" step, I was able to laugh at how my brain had constructed an elaborate firing scenario based on accidentally typing "pubic" instead of "public." (True story, unfortunately.)

Finding Your Inner Storm Chaser

Life gets chaotic. Your kid gets sick the same day as your big presentation, your basement floods during a family visit, and your car makes that expensive-sounding noise on the highway. These things happen whether you overthink them or not. The difference is whether you get swept away or find the calm in the center.

Here's how real humans (not Instagram yogis) stay centered when everything's falling apart:

- **Visualization that doesn't require artistic talent:** Picture yourself as a mountain. Weather happens around you—storms, sunshine, whatever—but the mountain remains. Cheesy? Yes. Effective when you're losing your mind? Also, yes.

- **Faith without the lecture:** If you've got a spiritual practice, lean on it. If you don't, that's cool too. The point is connecting to something bigger than your immediate problems, whether that's God, the universe, or just the realization that humans have been surviving chaos for thousands of years.

- **Thought renovation:** This is just a fancy way of saying "challenge your dramatic assumptions." When your brain screams, "This is the worst thing ever!" ask it for evidence. Has anything actually been "the worst thing ever" before? How did that turn out? Usually, we survive.

- **The positivity sandwich:** Between two slices of chaos, find one good thing happening. Your presentation bombed, but your hair looked amazing, and you didn't pass out from anxiety. Take the win where you can.

- **Control is mostly an illusion anyway:** Ever notice how the things we stress most about controlling are usually things we can't actually control? Other people's opinions, traffic, the weather, and whether your teenager makes good choices. Recognizing what's outside your control isn't giving up; it's focusing your energy where it actually matters.

- **Uncertainty is the only certainty:** The human brain hates not knowing. It would rather believe something terrible and certain than something unknown. But learning to sit with "I don't know what happens next" is like a superpower for overthinkers.

I remember when I tried to control my son's college application process and ended up with hives. I finally had to accept that checking the application portal seventeen times a day wouldn't change the outcome. The hives cleared up within a week of surrendering to the uncertainty.

Detaching from thoughts and staying centered aren't one-time achievements; they're practices. Some days you'll nail it, feeling all zen while chaos swirls. Other days you'll get sucked right into the tornado. That's not failure; it's being human. The goal isn't perfection; it's bouncing back faster each time. And sometimes, the most centered thing you can do is admit, "I'm not feeling very centered right now, and that's okay."

Part 4:

Living the New You—Moving Forward With Confidence

Chapter 12:

Creating a Life That Supports Balance

So, you've made it this far—congratulations! You've learned to recognize your thought spirals, interrupt them mid-spin, and even find moments of calm in the chaos. That's huge. But let's be honest: You're still living in the same life that created your overthinking habit in the first place.

It's like trying to quit sugar while working in a donut shop. Technically possible, but damn near impossible in practice.

I learned this lesson the hard way when I tried to reduce my anxiety while still maintaining five group chats that pinged 24-7, working for a boss who sent emails at 3 a.m., and living with a roommate who started political debates over breakfast. My therapist finally said, "You know, sometimes the problem isn't you; it's the water you're swimming in."

Your environment shapes your thinking more than any mindfulness app ever could. The people you spend time with, the physical spaces you inhabit, and the routines that structure your day—all of these things are either feeding your overthinking habit or starving it.

Designing Your Life: The Peaceful Mind Blueprint

Have you ever noticed how some spaces just feel right? You walk in and immediately breathe easier. Or how certain friends leave you energized while others drain every ounce of your mental battery? That's not random; it's the invisible architecture of your life at work.

You can actually design your life to quiet that overthinking mind of yours. I'm not talking about some complicated system that requires a PhD to implement. This is about simple, everyday choices that add up to major mental peace.

Start with your physical spaces. Look around your home or workspace right now. Does it make you feel calm or chaotic? Clutter isn't just visually distracting; it's mentally exhausting.

Your brain registers each item as something to potentially think about. That pile of unread mail? Your overthinking mind sees it as twenty different decisions waiting to be made.

You don't need to become a minimalist overnight (unless that's your thing). Just experiment with clearing one surface that you see daily. That nightstand drowning in random stuff? Clear it off, keep only what brings you peace, and watch how your bedtime overthinking might just ease up a bit.

Now, for the people part. We all have that friend who somehow turns every coffee date into a stress session. You know the one; they highlight every possible thing that could go wrong in any situation. While they might be lovely people, they're overthinking enablers.

Take a moment to mentally sort your relationships into three categories: energizers, neutrals, and drainers. The energizers leave you feeling lighter, more capable. The neutrals are fine either way. The drainers? They're the ones who send your thought spiral into overdrive.

I'm not suggesting you dramatically cut people off (though sometimes that's necessary). Instead, be intentional about exposure. Maybe that anxiety-inducing colleague doesn't need to be your lunch buddy five days a week. Perhaps your catastrophizing cousin is better in small doses. Surround yourself with people who help your mind settle rather than stir it up. Digital relationships count, too. That news site that leaves you convinced the world is ending? The social media account that makes you question every life choice? They're relationships, too, ones you can modify or end. I used to start every morning with twenty minutes of news scrolling.

No wonder my days began with worry! Now, I check headlines once, later in the day, and my mornings feel spacious instead of suffocating.

Then there's the magic of routine. Overthinking loves uncertainty; it's prime territory for your mind to explore every conceivable scenario. Creating gentle structures in your day reduces the mental load of constant decision-making.

This isn't about scheduling every minute. It's about creating predictable rhythms that your brain can relax into. Maybe it's a morning ritual of three deep breaths before checking your phone. Or a consistent bedtime that signals to your body it's time to power down.

I struggled with Sunday night insomnia for years, my mind racing with work worries. Creating a simple evening routine (shower, tea, ten minutes of reading something light) gave my brain the signal that it was time to transition.

The overthinking didn't disappear instantly, but it quieted considerably.

Your environment, relationships, and routines aren't just background features in your life; they're active ingredients in your mental well-being recipe. The beauty is that you get to be the chef. Mix, adjust, and taste-test until you find the combination that helps your mind find that sweet spot of clarity and peace.

Breaking Free: Nurturing Your Positive Mindset

You know that moment when you're doing great, feeling confident, and then—whoosh—you're right back where you started, overthinking everything again? Yeah, we've all been there.

Building Your Positive Mindset Toolkit

Your mindset is kind of like a garden. You can't just yank out the weeds (those negative thoughts) and walk away.

You've got to plant something good in their place, or those weeds come back faster than you can blink.

- **Start with your strengths:** We're weirdly good at cataloging everything we mess up, but terrible at remembering what we do well. Write down three things you're genuinely good at. Not world-changing stuff; maybe you make excellent coffee, remember people's birthdays, or can parallel park like a boss. These count.

- **Practice gratitude without the cheese:** I'm not talking about forced sunshine-and-rainbows gratitude. Find three real things each day that didn't completely suck. Your morning shower was hot. The traffic light turned green right when you got there. Your coworker didn't microwave fish in the break room again. Small wins matter.

- **Be your own best friend:** When you mess up, what do you tell yourself? If it's meaner than what you'd say to a friend in the same situation, you need to adjust your inner voice. Self-compassion isn't about lowering standards; it's about being reasonable with yourself.

- **Take care of the basics:** You can't think clearly when you're running on fumes. Sleep, food, movement, water. I know, I know—groundbreaking advice. But seriously, when did you last go to bed at a decent time without scrolling your phone until 2 a.m.?

- **Use positive affirmations that don't make you cringe:** Forget "I am a magnificent butterfly of success." Try something you actually believe: "I can handle whatever comes up today" or "I'm learning to trust myself more."

- **Stay in today:** Your brain loves time travel, replaying yesterday's awkward conversation or fast-forwarding to next month's presentation disaster. When you catch yourself drifting, bring your attention back to right now. What do you see, hear, and smell?

- **Redirect the negative spiral:** Notice when your thoughts start spiraling, then ask, "Is this helping me solve anything, or am I just rehearsing problems?" If it's the latter, do something else. Call someone, take a walk, organize your junk drawer, or whatever breaks the cycle.

- **Laugh at yourself (nicely):** Humor deflates anxiety better than almost anything. When I catch myself catastrophizing about sending a typo-filled email, I remind myself that no one's getting fired over "teh" instead of "the."

- **Choose your crowd carefully:** You know those friends who could find something wrong with winning the lottery? You love them, but maybe don't call them when you need a pep talk. Stick close to people who see what's possible, not just what could go wrong.

Staying on Track (Without Falling Into Old Traps)

Here's the thing about breaking habits: your brain doesn't like empty spaces.

If you just try to stop overthinking without replacing it with something else, you're basically creating a vacuum that your old patterns will rush to fill.

- **Replace, don't just erase:** When you feel the urge to spiral, have a replacement ready. Instead of mentally rehearsing every possible disaster, write down what you know for sure right now. Instead of analyzing that text message for the fifteenth time, text someone else about something completely different.

- **Redefine what success looks like:** Success isn't never having anxious thoughts; it's catching them sooner and bouncing back faster. Some days, success is only spiraling for ten minutes instead of two hours. That's progress.

- **Know your triggers and have an escape plan:** Maybe it's certain topics, times of day, or even particular rooms where you tend to overthink. You don't have to avoid everything forever, but knowing your weak spots helps you prepare.

- **Use your crew:** That support group you've been putting together? Actually lean on them. Not just when everything's falling apart, but for regular reality checks. Sometimes just saying out loud, "I'm going down the rabbit hole about work again," is enough to snap you out of it.

Change isn't a straight line; it's more like a drunk person trying to walk home. Sometimes you make progress, sometimes you bump into things, but you usually get there eventually.

Goals That Don't Make You Want to Hide Under a Blanket

Let's talk about goals for a minute. Not the kind you set on New Year's Eve after three glasses of champagne, where you decide you're going to run a marathon, learn French, and reorganize your entire life by February. I'm talking about the kind of goals that don't make you break out in a cold sweat every time you think about them.

You know what happens when we set crazy goals that have nothing to do with who we actually are? We overthink them to death. We lie awake at 2 a.m., wondering why we're not jogging at 5 a.m. like we said we would or why we haven't touched that guitar that's been collecting dust for three months.

Start With What Actually Matters to You

Before you even think about what you want to achieve, you need to get honest about what you care about. And I mean really care about, not what you think you should care about, because your sister's friend posted about it on Instagram. Sit down somewhere quiet (yes, the bathroom counts) and ask yourself, *What makes me feel good about myself?* Not accomplished or impressive—just good. Maybe it's making people laugh. Maybe it's having a clean kitchen. Maybe it's knowing random facts about penguins. Whatever it is, that's your starting point.

I spent years setting goals around being more "productive" because that seemed important. Turns out, I don't actually care about productivity. I care about having time to read weird books and take long walks. Once I figured that out, everything got easier.

Your values aren't a Pinterest board of inspirational quotes. They're the stuff that makes you feel like yourself when you're doing it.

Check Your Energy Account

Here's something they don't teach you in those goal-setting workshops: You can't spend energy you don't have. I know, revolutionary concept.

Think about your energy like a bank account. Some things make deposits; maybe that's time alone, or being outside, or talking to your best friend. Other things make withdrawals: difficult conversations, crowded places, or trying to adult before you've had coffee.

If you set a goal that requires more withdrawals than you've got deposits coming in, you're going to burn out. And then you're going to overthink why you can't stick to anything and what's wrong with you. (Spoiler alert: Nothing's wrong with you.) Look at your typical week. When do you feel energized? When do you feel drained? Don't try to force yourself into someone else's schedule. If you're not a morning person, stop setting goals that require you to be chipper at dawn. Work with what you've got, not against it.

Make Goals That Don't Stress You Out

Good goals should feel exciting, not terrifying. If thinking about your goal makes you want to take a nap, it's probably not the right goal for you right now.

Start smaller than you think you need to. Seriously. If you want to exercise more, don't commit to an hour at the gym every day. Commit to putting on your sneakers three times a week. That's it. You can always do more once you get there, but you can't do less than nothing.

The goal is to build momentum, not to impress anyone. I once set a goal to "drink more water" and started by just keeping a water bottle on my desk. Revolutionary? No. Sustainable? Absolutely.

Keep It Real With Yourself

Your goals need to fit your actual life, not the life you wish you had. If you've got three kids under five, your goal probably shouldn't be "meditate for an hour every morning." Maybe it's "Take three deep breaths before I lose my patience with someone."

This isn't about lowering your standards. It's about being smart about where you are right now. You can always adjust as things change, but you've got to start from reality.

Also, check in with yourself regularly. Not in a judgy way, but like you're checking in with a friend. How's this going? Does this still make sense? Do we need to switch things up?

The Overthinking Escape Hatch

When you start spiraling about whether you're doing enough or the right things, remember this: The perfect goal doesn't exist. There are just goals that work for you right now and goals that don't. If a goal is making you miserable, change it. You're not signing a contract with the universe. You're just trying stuff out to see what sticks.

Your goals should help you feel more like yourself, not less. If they're doing the opposite, it's time for a reset.

Chapter 13:

The Role of Gratitude and Positive Thinking

You've probably heard someone tell you to "have an attitude of gratitude," and chances are good you rolled your eyes so hard they nearly fell out of your head. I get it. I really do.

There's something about gratitude advice that makes it sound like it came straight from a motivational poster featuring a kitten hanging from a tree branch. It feels cheesy, forced, and about as helpful as being told to "just think positive" when you're having the worst day of your life.

But here's the thing, and I hate to be the bearer of news that sounds like it came from your overly optimistic aunt: There's actually some real wisdom buried under all that flowery language. Don't worry, I'm not about to tell you to start every morning by thanking the universe for your blessings while doing yoga in flowing white clothes.

The Great Mental U-Turn: How Gratitude Stops the Spiral

It's Tuesday, you're lying in bed at 2 a.m., and your brain decides now's the perfect time to replay that cringeworthy thing you said at work six months ago. Then it jumps to wondering if your boss thinks you're totally incompetent, which somehow spirals into imagining yourself getting fired, which ends up with you living in a cardboard box, eating ramen.

You know how it goes.

The Art of the Mental U-Turn

When your brain gets stuck in one of those loops, it's like a broken record that keeps skipping on the same terrible song. You keep hearing the same awful notes over and over, getting more frustrated each time, but you can't seem to make it stop.

Gratitude is like walking over and lifting the needle off that record. It doesn't fix the scratch, but at least you don't have to keep listening to the same depressing chorus on repeat. It's not magic, and it's not about ignoring your real problems. It's about giving your brain something else to chew on when it gets stuck replaying the same old disasters.

When you catch yourself going down one of those dark paths, instead of continuing the slide, you force yourself to change direction. If your brain is going "This presentation is going to bomb, and everyone will think I'm clueless," you jump in with, "Actually, I'm glad I get to talk about something I care about with people who might actually find it interesting."

It's not about fooling yourself. It's about showing your brain that the same situation can look completely different depending on where you focus.

Breaking the Worry Habit

Your brain loves doing the same thing over and over. It's like that friend who's been ordering chicken parmesan at every Italian restaurant for the past ten years because "I know I like it." Except in this case, what your brain "likes" is actually making you miserable; it's just familiar. When you worry about the same stuff repeatedly, you're teaching your brain to be a world-class worrier about that particular thing. It becomes your go-to response.

The boss wants to see you? Obviously, you're in trouble. Does your friend take a while to text back? They must be mad at you.

Gratitude works because it teaches your brain a different habit. Instead of jumping straight to the worst possible outcome, you train it to look around for something else first. It's like teaching your paranoid brain that not every creaky sound at night means someone's breaking in; sometimes it's just the house settling.

From What-If to What-Is

Your overthinking brain lives in what-if land. What if this goes wrong? What if they think I'm weird? What if I screw up? What if, what if, what if? It's like having a roommate who only talks about potential disasters.

Gratitude drags you back to right now. What's actually going okay today? What's working in your life at this moment? What do you have now that you were hoping for last year?

I'm not talking about forcing yourself to be grateful for stuff you genuinely hate. If your job sucks, you don't have to be thankful for it. But maybe you can be grateful that it pays for your morning coffee, or that your coworker makes you laugh, or that you learned something new this week.

The Confidence Connection

Here's something interesting: When you regularly practice looking for what's going right, you start to trust yourself more. It's like you're building a file in your brain labeled "Evidence That I Can Handle Things" instead of just the one labeled "All The Ways This Could Go Wrong." Every time you catch something you're grateful for, even tiny stuff like "I'm glad I remembered to charge my phone last night," you're basically building up evidence that says, "Hey, look, sometimes things actually work out okay. I'm not completely hopeless at this life thing."

This isn't about becoming annoyingly positive. It's about balance. If your brain spends all day looking for problems, of course, you're going to feel anxious and overwhelmed. But if you also spend some time noticing what's working, you start to feel more capable of handling whatever comes up.

Making It Real (Not Fake)

The key to using gratitude as a loop-breaker is keeping it real. Don't try to be grateful for things that genuinely upset you; that's just another form of lying to yourself. Instead, look for the small, true things that you actually do appreciate.

Maybe you're stressed about money, but you're grateful your friend listened to you vent about it. Maybe work is crazy, but you're glad you figured out how to use that new software.

Maybe your day was mostly lousy, but that sandwich you had for lunch was actually pretty great.

Small Moves, Big Changes: Your Daily Gratitude Toolkit

Let's talk about actually doing this gratitude thing instead of just thinking about it.

Start Before Your Feet Hit the Floor

Your brain is actually pretty mellow first thing in the morning, before it starts its daily freakout about everything you need to do. While you're still lying there dreading getting up, use this brief window of calm.

Think of five things you're grateful for. And I mean really simple stuff, not "I'm grateful for the gift of life," unless you genuinely feel that way. More like "I'm glad my bed is warm" or "I'm grateful I don't have to be anywhere for another twenty minutes."

Some days it might be, "I'm grateful my upstairs neighbor finally stopped playing music at 2 a.m." Other days it could be, "I'm glad I remembered to plug in my phone last night." The point isn't to find life-changing gratitude; it's to start your day noticing a few things that don't completely suck.

Write It Down (But Keep It Real)

Gratitude journals get a bad rap because people think they need to write beautiful, meaningful entries every day. Screw that. Your gratitude list can be a sticky note on your bathroom mirror or something you type into your phone.

Write down one thing that didn't suck about your day. Maybe your coffee was actually good for once. Maybe someone let you merge in traffic without honking. Maybe you found a parking spot right away. These tiny wins count just as much as the big stuff.

Notice the People Around You

This one's sneaky good for stopping overthinking because it pulls you out of your own head. When someone holds a door for you, actually make eye contact and say thanks. When the cleaning person at work does something nice, let them know you noticed.

It sounds tiny, but here's what happens: Instead of spending those moments stressing about your endless to-do list or replaying some cringey conversation, you're actually connecting with another person.

Your brain gets a break from running in circles. Plus, people remember when you actually see them. That cleaning person you thanked might be the one who helps you find your keys when you drop them later. The world feels a little less like everyone's just ignoring each other.

Get Outside Your Head (Literally)

When you're stuck spinning your wheels about something, go outside if you can. Not for some big nature moment, just step outside and notice one thing. How the light looks different than it did this morning.

How the air smells like rain or food from someone's kitchen. The fact that there are birds just doing their thing, completely unbothered by whatever's eating at you.

I'm not saying fresh air is going to fix everything. But it's hard to catastrophize about next week's meeting when you're watching a squirrel completely blow it trying to jump between trees. Sometimes you just need the reminder that the world is way bigger than whatever's bugging you.

Switch Up Your Phone Calls

Instead of calling someone to complain about how everything's going wrong (which we all do, and that's totally fine sometimes), try calling someone just to tell them something you like about them. It doesn't have to be deep. "Hey, I was just thinking about how you always remember to ask about my annoying boss situation," works perfectly.

This completely flips how your day feels. Instead of going over all your problems, you're actively hunting for good stuff to share. Your brain starts looking for positives instead of just scanning for disasters.

The Poetry Trick

You don't have to write good poetry. You don't even have to show it to anyone. But trying to put something you're grateful for into a few lines makes your brain actually focus on it instead of just breezing past.

"The coffee shop guy remembered my order / Made my Tuesday feel less like a chore" isn't going to win any awards, but it made me stop and actually think about how nice that moment was instead of rushing past it.

How Gratitude Rewires Your Overthinking Mind

Remember when your grandmother told you to "count your blessings?" Turns out, Grandma was right. She just didn't know she was giving you brain medicine.

The Overthinking Brain vs. The Grateful Brain

When you're stuck in overthinking mode, your brain looks like a traffic jam during rush hour. The prefrontal cortex, which is your thinking center, goes into overdrive, burning through mental energy like a gas-guzzling SUV. Meanwhile, your amygdala (the brain's alarm system) stays on high alert, convinced that thinking harder will somehow solve everything.

But here's where gratitude comes in like a traffic cop with a magic wand.

When you genuinely feel grateful, your brain does something cool. It dumps a bunch of feel-good chemicals: dopamine, serotonin, and oxytocin. These are like your brain's natural happy pills. Dopamine makes you feel good, serotonin lifts your mood, and oxytocin helps you chill out. This chemical rush does what your overthinking brain needs most; it makes everything stop for a minute.

The Default Mode Network: Your Brain's Screensaver

Scientists have discovered something called the default mode network (DMN) (Yeshurun et al., 2021). This is what your brain does when it's supposed to be "resting," except it's not really resting at all. It's ruminating, worrying, and running through scenarios like a broken record. For overthinkers, the DMN is like having a radio stuck between stations—lots of noise, no clear signal. Gratitude practices change how this network works. People who say "thank you" regularly have quieter minds. Less mental noise, fewer worry spirals, and actual calm.

Rewiring the Worry Highway

Your brain has neural pathways; think of them as well-worn hiking trails. The more you use a trail, the more established it becomes. Overthinkers have created superhighways for worry and rumination. Every time you spiral into "what if" thinking, you're strengthening those worry roads.

Gratitude creates new pathways. Each time you notice something you're thankful for, you're literally building new neural real estate. At first, these gratitude pathways are like tiny footpaths. But with practice, they become strong enough to redirect traffic away from the worry superhighway.

The Attention Hijack

Here's one of gratitude's best tricks: It steals your attention. Overthinking happens because your mind gets stuck on problems, spinning them around endlessly. Gratitude grabs your attention away from problems and points it toward what's actually okay.

This isn't about pretending problems don't exist. It's about giving your brain a breather so it can actually solve problems instead of just worrying about them.

The Stress Response Reboot

Chronic overthinking keeps your stress response system stuck in the "on" position. Your cortisol levels stay elevated, your nervous system remains activated, and your brain thinks you're constantly under threat.

Gratitude turns on your rest and digest mode. It's like switching your brain from panic mode back to normal. Your heart slows down, you breathe easier, and that tight feeling in your chest lets up.

Making It Stick

What I love about gratitude is that you can't mess it up. You don't need to feel thankful for huge, life-changing stuff every day. Sometimes it's just being glad your coffee didn't suck or that your dog did something adorable.

Your brain doesn't care if what you're grateful for is deep or silly. It just wants you building those new pathways, one "thanks" at a time.

Chapter 14:

Embracing the Flow of Life

Ever notice how some days just... work? You're crushing your to-do list, conversations feel effortless, and even traffic lights turn green as you approach. Then there are the other days, when you spill coffee on your shirt, forget your password for the seventeenth time, and every email feels like defusing a bomb.

The difference isn't luck. It's flow.

What the Hell Is "Flow" Anyway?

If "finding your flow" sounds like something your yoga teacher's yoga teacher would say while standing on her head and sipping kombucha, I get it. But stick with me here.

Remember that basketball game where you couldn't miss a shot? Or that work presentation where the words just came to you? Or even that road trip where four hours felt like twenty minutes because the conversation was so good? That's flow.

Flow is when you're so wrapped up in what you're doing that you forget to check your phone, worry about how you look, or mentally rehearse everything you need to do tomorrow. It's being completely here, now, doing this thing.

It is the sweet spot where your skills match the challenge perfectly, not so easy you're bored, not so hard you're freaking out. But I like to think of it as the mental equivalent of those perfect jeans that make your butt look amazing and are still comfortable enough to eat a burrito in.

The Overthinking Kryptonite

For those of us with brains that run on premium-grade anxiety, flow is like kryptonite to overthinking. When you're in flow, there's no mental bandwidth left for your greatest hits album of worries. Your internal narrator finally shuts the hell up.

Here's the beautiful irony: Flow happens precisely when you stop trying to control everything. It's surrendering to the current moment instead of frantically paddling upstream against it.

Take my friend Jake. He spent three months obsessing over asking for a raise, planning exactly what to say, and anticipating every possible objection his boss might have. When the big day came, he was so in his head that he tripped over his rehearsed script and left feeling like he'd bombed. Two weeks later, he had an impromptu conversation with the same boss about a successful project, wasn't overthinking it at all, and casually mentioned his contributions. Boom, got the raise on the spot.

The universe has a sick sense of humor that way.

Finding Your Flow (Without Moving to Bali)

So, how do you find this magical state without quitting your job to "find yourself" abroad? (Though if you can swing that financially, no judgment here.)

First, recognize that flow isn't one-size-fits-all. My flow state comes from writing or hiking. My partner finds it gaming. My mom gets it gardening. The activity doesn't matter; what matters is it's challenging enough to demand your full attention but familiar enough that you're not constantly stopping to figure out what to do next.

Here are some training wheels for your flow bicycle:

- **Physical stuff works wonders:** Running, swimming, yoga—anything that forces you to be in your body instead of just your head. I was skeptical until I tried lap swimming and realized I'd gone 30 minutes without a single thought about my work deadlines or that weird thing my friend said last week. Just me, counting laps, and trying not to drown. Bliss.

- **Set clear goals, but then forget about them:** Sounds contradictory, right? But flow needs direction without obsession. Know what you're aiming for, then focus on the process rather than constantly checking if you're "there yet," like a kid on a road trip.

- **Get familiar with the territory:** Flow happens more easily with tasks you know well enough to navigate confidently. That's why beginners rarely experience it; they're still at the "Wait, how do I hold this again?" stage. Stick with something long enough to get past the awkward phase.

- **Meditation isn't just for people who own singing bowls:** Even five minutes of focusing on your breath trains your brain to stay in the moment rather than time-traveling to past regrets or future catastrophes. And no, your thoughts won't magically stop. My meditation sessions still involve mentally redecorating my bathroom and remembering embarrassing moments from high school. The point isn't having zero thoughts; it's noticing when you're drifting and gently coming back.

- **Find your creative outlet:** Remember finger painting as a kid before you cared if it was "good"? Channel that energy. Write terrible poetry. Make ugly pottery. Cook experimental meals that sometimes fail spectacularly. Creating without judgment is flow's natural habitat.

Staying in Flow When Life Gets Stormy

"This is all great," you might be thinking, "but clearly you haven't met my boss/children/mortgage."

Fair point. Finding flow during life's highlight reel is one thing. Maintaining it when everything's falling apart is black-belt level.

But here's the secret: Challenging times are actually when flow becomes most valuable and, sometimes, most accessible.

When my dad was in the hospital last year, I found unexpected moments of flow sitting with him, just focusing on the rhythm of turning the pages in my book, the sound of his breathing, and the sunlight moving across the floor. Not because I was trying to escape reality, but because I was fully in it, without the added layer of anxious thoughts about what might happen next.

In crisis, our brains naturally narrow our focus to what's directly in front of us. The overthinking part gets temporarily sidelined by necessity. It's why people often report a strange clarity during emergencies.

You can cultivate this crisis-clarity without waiting for emergencies:

- **Bring it back to your body:** Feel your feet on the floor. Notice your breathing. Touch something and really feel its texture. Your body only exists in the present, so it's your anchor when your mind wants to time-travel.

- **Shrink the timeframe:** When everything feels overwhelming, focus on just the next hour, the next ten minutes, or even just the next breath. Flow doesn't require long stretches; it can happen in moments.

- **Embrace the suck:** Sometimes flow isn't about feeling good; it's about being fully present even with difficult emotions. Feeling the sadness or fear without adding a layer of thoughts about the feeling.

Flow isn't about having a perfect life. It's about being fully in the life you have, messy, uncertain, and occasionally wonderful. It's about trading the exhausting job of trying to control everything for the relief of riding whatever wave comes your way.

And for chronic overthinkers, that trade is the best deal going.

Chapter 15:

Living Your Life With Vitality

Remember that scene in The Wizard of Oz when everything suddenly shifts from black and white to Technicolor? That's what breaking free from overthinking feels like. The same life, but suddenly vibrant, dimensional, and way more interesting.

If you've stuck with me through fourteen chapters of untangling your mental knots, you're probably starting to experience some of those color bursts already. Maybe you've caught yourself actually enjoying a meal instead of mentally rehearsing tomorrow's meeting while you eat. Or perhaps you've gone a whole day without creating an elaborate disaster scenario based on a single ambiguous text message. Progress!

But here's the thing about overthinking: It's not just a mental habit. It's a whole-body experience that affects everything from your sleep to your digestion to that weird tension headache you get every Tuesday. The flip side is also true: When you calm your pinball-machine mind, your entire system benefits.

Let's talk about how all these pieces fit together and how to keep this momentum going long after you've used this book as a coaster for your third cup of coffee.

Your Brain and Body Are Actually Roommates

For years, we've treated physical health and mental health like they're living in separate apartments, maybe waving occasionally in the hallway. "Oh hey, anxiety! How's it going? Cool, cool. Well, I'm off to the cardiologist—see ya!" Turns out, they're actually sharing the same studio apartment and fighting over the thermostat.

My cousin Mark is a total health nut—he ran marathons, ate like he was auditioning for a kale commercial, and had the abs to prove it. But he was also the king of catastrophic thinking. Every minor work issue was the end of his career; every slight disagreement with his girlfriend was proof they were doomed.

Despite his peak physical condition, Mark developed chronic acid reflux, mysterious skin rashes, and insomnia that no amount of melatonin could touch. His doctor ran every test in the book before finally asking, "So... how's your stress level?"

Medical science is finally catching up to what our bodies have known all along: Your thoughts directly impact your physical health. When you're stuck in overthinking mode, your body is constantly flooded with stress hormones. Your heart works harder, your immune system gets suppressed, your digestion goes haywire, and your energy tanks faster than my phone battery on a road trip.

This isn't just woo-woo wellness talk. Hard-nosed cardiologists now routinely screen heart patients for anxiety and depression because the connection is that strong. One study found that people with high anxiety had a 48% higher risk of heart issues, about the same increased risk as being a heavy smoker (Roest et al., 2010). Yikes.

But before you start overthinking about your overthinking (meta-anxiety, anyone?), remember the reverse is also true: Reducing mental stress creates measurable physical benefits. Your blood pressure drops. Your sleep improves.

Your immune system perks up like a dog hearing the treat drawer open.

The Vitality Trifecta

Think of vitality as a three-legged stool: physical health, mental clarity, and emotional well-being. Kick out any leg, and you're going to have a hard time staying upright.

1. **Physical vitality** isn't just about having abs you could grate cheese on. It's about having enough energy to do the things that matter to you, whether that's chasing your kids around the yard or simply making it through a workday without mainlining caffeine. Basic stuff like moving your body regularly, eating food that doesn't make you feel like garbage, and getting enough sleep creates the foundation for everything else.

2. **Mental clarity** is what we've focused on throughout this book; the ability to think without your thoughts thinking you. It's recognizing when you're catastrophizing and being able to say, "Thanks, but no thanks" to that disaster movie your brain is trying to produce and direct.

3. **Emotional well-being** is perhaps the trickiest piece, allowing yourself to feel your feelings without drowning in them or stuffing them in the basement until they stage a midnight rebellion. It's the difference between "I'm feeling anxious" and "I am anxiety personified and doomed to eternal suffering."

When all three are working together, that's when life gets juicy. That's vitality.

From Surviving to Thriving: Your Owner's Manual

So, how do you maintain this delicate ecosystem once you've started to establish it?

Here's your no-BS maintenance guide:

- **Schedule worry-free zones:** Just like you might have a "no phones at dinner" rule, create pockets of your day that are overthinking-free. Maybe it's your morning shower, your commute, or the first cup of coffee. Train your brain that these times are sacred.

- **Move your meat suit daily:** Your body was designed to move, not hunch over a laptop for 10 hours. Find something that feels good—walking, dancing in your kitchen, chasing your dog around the yard, whatever—and do it regularly.

- **Feed yourself like you'd feed someone you actually like:** No, you don't need to become a clean-eating guru who makes their own nut milk. Just aim for food that gives you energy rather than making you want to nap under your desk. Your brain uses about 20% of your body's energy; it needs good fuel, not just whatever was available at the gas station.

- **Create a connection that doesn't require overthinking:** Some relationships feel like walking through an emotional minefield; one wrong word and boom. Other connections feel like coming home. Prioritize the people who don't require mental gymnastics just to have a conversation.

- **Remember that setbacks aren't failures:** You will absolutely have days when your mind goes full hurricane mode again. That doesn't mean you've failed or that this whole journey was pointless. It means you're human. The difference now is that you know how to find your way back to calm without getting lost for months.

When I finally broke my own overthinking habit, the most surprising change wasn't the improved sleep or even the reduction in those tension headaches that felt like wearing a too-tight headband. It was how much more room there was in my life. Room for spontaneous joy. Room for actual, deep-breath relaxation. Room for being present with the people I love instead of mentally preparing rebuttals to arguments that hadn't happened.

That's the real gift waiting on the other side of overthinking, not just the absence of mental chaos, but the presence of genuine vitality. Your life, in Technicolor.

Conclusion

So, here we are at the end of our little adventure together. If you've made it this far, you've probably dog-eared some pages, highlighted a few passages that hit too close to home, and maybe even tried some of the strategies we've talked about. Maybe you've caught yourself mid-spiral and thought, "Oh hey, I'm doing that overthinking thing again." Progress!

Let's be real: You're not going to close this book and suddenly transform into one of those mystical creatures who "just don't worry about things they can't control." Those people—do they even exist? Are they robots? The investigation continues.

Your brain isn't going to magically stop generating worst-case scenarios or replaying awkward conversations from 2014. That's not the goal here. The goal was never to stop thinking entirely, despite what my seventh-grade teacher suggested when she wrote "stop thinking so much" on my report card. Thanks, Mrs. Peterson, super helpful.

The actual goal is much simpler and much deeper: to stop being held hostage by those thoughts.

Remember where we started? With that familiar feeling of being trapped in a mental maze of your own creation. The exhaustion of rehearsing conversations that never happen. The physical tension of carrying tomorrow's problems in today's body. The relationships were strained because you were physically present but mentally lost in the labyrinth.

I'm not going to pretend that reading one book solves all that. No single tool or technique is a magic bullet. But what you have now is a toolbox.

Some days, you'll need the heavy-duty notice and name hammer for those persistent thought patterns. And some days, you'll forget the whole damn toolbox and find yourself three hours deep into an anxiety spiral about something someone might have implied about you at work.

That's not failure. That's being human.

The difference now is that you know the way back. You recognize the signs when your thoughts start to hijack your peace. You have practices to bring yourself back to the present moment. And most importantly, you understand that you are not your thoughts; you're the awareness behind them, the one who can choose whether to believe the stories your mind tells.

I still remember the first time I really got this. I was lying awake at 3 a.m., as one does, mentally drafting and redrafting an email to a client. I'd been at it for over an hour when suddenly I had this moment of clarity: "Wait, I'm not actually writing this email right now. I'm just torturing myself with hypothetical versions of it." I started laughing right there in the dark. The spell was broken.

Did I never overthink an email again? Please. I'm overthinking this very conclusion as I write it. But that moment changed something fundamental; I recognized the pattern. And once you can see the walls of the maze, you're already on your way out.

As you close this book and return to your life, with all its deadlines, relationships, and uncertainties, my hope for you isn't perfection. It's perspective. The ability to step back and see your thoughts as weather passing through the sky of your awareness, not as commands you must obey or truths you must believe. Your life is happening right now, not in the rehearsals and reviews your mind is staging.

It's in the taste of your morning coffee. The feeling of your kid's hand in yours. The satisfaction of solving a problem at work. The simple pleasure of a hot shower after a long day.

All the time you've spent overthinking isn't wasted if it led you here, to this new awareness. Think of it as the price of admission to a more present life. A life where you still think—deeply, creatively, meaningfully—but where thinking serves you rather than enslaves you.

Your thoughts will always be there, running commentary like an overenthusiastic sports announcer. But now you know you can turn down the volume, switch channels, or sometimes just mute the broadcast entirely and enjoy the game.

So, here's to fewer sleepless nights, less second-guessing, and more actually living the one wild and precious life you have.

Your overthinking mind brought you to this book. Your wiser self will take it from here.

References

Ackerman, C. E. (2018, February 12). *Cognitive restructuring techniques for reframing thoughts.* Positive Psychology. https://positivepsychology.com/cbt-cognitive-restructuring-cognitive-distortions/#worksheets-cognitive-restructuring

Ackerman, C. E. (2024a, August 3). *23 amazing health benefits of mindfulness for body and brain.* Positive Psychology. https://positivepsychology.com/benefits-of-mindfulness/

Ackerman, C. E. (2024b, September 17). *Mindfulness-based stress reduction: The ultimate MBSR guide.* Positive Psychology. https://positivepsychology.com/mindfulness-based-stress-reduction-mbsr/

Anwar, Y. (2017, September 7). *How many different human emotions are there?* Greater Good Magazine. https://greatergood.berkeley.edu/article/item/how_many_different_human_emotions_are_there

Anxiety disorders—facts & statistics. (2022, October 28). Anxiety and Depression Association of America. https://adaa.org/understanding-anxiety/facts-statistics

Bardo, N. (2022, January 9). *Silencing your inner critic: A beginner's guide.* It's All You Boo. https://itsallyouboo.com/silencing-your-inner-critic/

Bernhard, T. (2011, June 6). *6 benefits of practicing mindfulness outside of meditation.* Psychology Today. https://www.psychologytoday.com/us/blog/turnin g-straw-gold/201106/6-benefits-practicing-mindfulness-outside-meditation

Bernhard, T. (2014, June 5). *7 myths about mindfulness.* Psychology Today. https://www.psychologytoday.com/us/blog/turnin g-straw-gold/201406/7-myths-about-mindfulness

Bhandari, T. (2023, April 19). *Mind-body connection is built into brain.* ScienceDaily. https://www.sciencedaily.com/releases/2023/04/2 30419125052.htm#google_vignette

Brown, H. (2024, July 26). *What is emotional intelligence? +18 ways to improve it* . Positive Psychology. https://positivepsychology.com/emotional-intelligence-eq/

Cash, E., Salmon, P., Weissbecker, I., Rebholz, W. N., Bayley-Veloso, R., Zimmaro, L., Floyd, A., Dedert, E., & Sephton, S. E. (2015). Mindfulness meditation alleviates fibromyalgia symptoms in women: Results of a randomized clinical trial. *Annals of Behavioral Medicine: A Publication of the Society of Behavioral Medicine,* *49*(3), 319–330. https://doi.org/10.1007/s12160-014-9665-0

Cassata, C. (2021, June 9). *10 areas that mindfulness & meditation make us better.* Psych Central. https://psychcentral.com/blog/surprising-health-benefits-of-mindfulness-meditation

Ceruto, S. (2024, October 23). *How overthinking in relationships can destroy your connection & how to break the cycle.* MindLAB. https://mindlabneuroscience.com/overthinking-in-relationships-destroy-connection/

Challenging negative thinking. (n.d.). MindWell. https://www.mindwell-leeds.org.uk/myself/exploring-your-mental-health/depression/challenging-negative-thinking/

Cherry, K. (2022, September 2). *Benefits of mindfulness.* Verywell Mind. https://www.verywellmind.com/the-benefits-of-mindfulness-5205137

Cherry, K. (2024, July 14). *The 6 types of basic emotions and their effect on human behavior.* Verywell Mind. https://www.verywellmind.com/an-overview-of-the-types-of-emotions-4163976

Christian, K. (2021, September 16). *What is embodiment & how can we use it for self-care?* The Good Trade. https://www.thegoodtrade.com/features/embodiment-definition/

Claude Steiner biography. (2015, August 9). Eric Berne M.D. https://ericberne.com/claude-steiner-biography/

Cleveland Clinic. (2022, May 15). *Overthinking disorder: Is it a mental illness?* Cleveland Clinic. https://health.clevelandclinic.org/is-overthinking-a-mental-illness

Cornyn-Selby, A. (n.d.). *Alyce Cornyn-Selby quotes*. A-Z Quotes. https://www.azquotes.com/author/64065-Alyce_Cornyn_Selby

Cox, J. (2022, November 15). *7 ways to overcome perfectionism*. Psych Central.

https://psychcentral.com/health/steps-to-conquer-perfectionism

Davidson, R. J., & Lutz, A. (2008). Buddha's brain: Neuroplasticity and meditation. *IEEE Signal Processing Magazine*, *25*(1), 176–174. https://www.ncbi.nlm.nih.gov/pmc/articles/PMC2944261/

Davis, T. (2021, May 18). *9 ways to cultivate a positive mindset*. Psychology Today. https://www.psychologytoday.com/us/blog/click-here-for-happiness/202105/9-ways-to-cultivate-a-positive-mindset

Dibdin, E. (2022a, March 29). *Need to control everything? This may be why*. Psych Central. https://psychcentral.com/blog/why-you-need-to-control-everything

Dibdin, E. (2022b, March 31). *The mental health benefits of journaling*. Psych Central. https://psychcentral.com/lib/the-health-benefits-of-journaling

Dina. (2019, October 31). *10 surprising exercises to improve mindfulness*. HubPages.

https://discover.hubpages.com/health/Mindfulness
-Exercises-You-Never-Tried

Disney, W. (n.d.). *Walt Disney quotes*. A-Z Quotes.
https://www.azquotes.com/author/4000-
Walt_Disney/tag/imagination

Dostoyevsky, F., MacAndrew, A. R., & Marcus, B. (2004).
*Notes from underground, White nights, The dream of a
ridiculous man, and Selections from the house of the dead*
(150th Anniversary Edition). Signet Classics.
(Original work published 1862)

Dr. Amit Ray biography. (2023, April 3). Dr. Amit Ray.
https://amitray.com/amitray-biography/

Dunham, W. (2023). Scientists identify mind-body nexus in
human brain. In *Reuters*.
https://www.reuters.com/lifestyle/science/scientist
s-identify-mind-body-nexus-human-brain-2023-04-
19/

Eddins, R. (2022, May 4). *Working with your inner critic*. Eddins
Counseling   Group.
https://eddinscounseling.com/working-with-your-
inner-critic/

Einstein, A. (n.d.-a). *Albert Einstein quotes*. Quotation.io.
https://quotation.io/quote/cant-solve-problems-
using-kind-thinking

Einstein, A. (n.d.-b). *Albert Einstein quotes*. BrainyQuote.
https://www.brainyquote.com/quotes/albert_einste
in_121643

Eliaz, I. (2022, September 21). *Break free from chronic stress cycle—with nature's help.* Isaac Eliaz MD. https://dreliaz.org/break-free-from-the-chronic-stress-cycle-with-natures-most-powerful-herbs/

Emde, A. (2023, June 12). *How to write your goals for a balanced life.* Lifestyle Anytime. https://lifestyleanytime.com.au/how-to-write-down-your-goals-for-a-balanced-life/

Engebretson, P. (2021, February 12). *How to stop overthinking everything: Close your open question loops - i'm busy being awesome.* I'm Busy Being Awesome. https://imbusybeingawesome.com/open-question-loops/

Epictetus. (n.d.-a). *Epictetus quotes.* A-Z Quotes. https://www.azquotes.com/quote/90291?ref=com munication

Epictetus. (n.d.-b). *Epictetus quotes.* Goodreads. https://www.goodreads.com/quotes/7588248-we-cannot-choose-our-external-circumstances-but-we-can-always

Estrada, J., & Lucas, C. (2024, May 17). *10 ways to regulate your nervous system, according to a brain and behavior experts.* Well+Good. https://www.wellandgood.com/regulate-your-nervous-system/

Evans, L. (2014, September 24). *You aren't imagining it: Email is making you more stressed out.* Fast Company. https://www.fastcompany.com/3036061/youarent-imagining-it-email-is-making-you-more-stressed-out

Expert Panel. (2022, April 29). 15 steps to get rid of negative thought patterns. *Forbes*. https://www.forbes.com/councils/forbescoachesco uncil/2022/04/28/15-steps-to-get-rid-of-negative-thought-patterns/

Fain, S., & Cahn, S. (1953). *You can fly! You can fly! You can fly!* Peter Pan Original Motion Picture Soundtrack. Walt Disney Records. https://genius.com/The-jud-conlon-chorus-you-can-fly-you-can-fly-you-can-fly-lyrics

Farris, M. (2022, July 13). *How to manage difficult emotions*. Counseling Recovery. https://www.counselingrecovery.com/blog-san-jose/-feel-your-feelings

Feldman Barrett, L. (2024, August 8). *Simplistic "fight or flight" idea undervalues the brain's predictive powers*. Scientific American. https://www.scientificamerican.com/article/simplis tic-fight-or-flight-idea-undervalues-the-brains-predictive-powers/

Forbes Coaches Council. (2021, December 10). 16 essential strategies to improve your decision-making skills. *Forbes*.

https://www.forbes.com/councils/forbescoachescouncil/20 20/05/28/16-essential-strategies-to-improve-your-decision-making-skills/

Frick, W. (2018, January 22). *3 ways to improve your decision making.* Harvard Business Review. https://hbr.org/2018/01/3-ways-to-improve-your-decision-making

Frontiers of the Mind. (2023, February 1). National Institute of Health National Library of Medicine. https://www.nlm.nih.gov/exhibition/emotions-and-disease/index.html#section6

Getting started with mindfulness. (n.d.). Mindful. https://www.mindful.org/meditation/mindfulness-getting-started/

Gibbons, E. (2023). The surprising benefit of meditative walks. *Nature.* https://doi.org/10.1038/d41586-023-01894-1

Godkin, S. (2020, April 5). *Self-Compassion or self-criticism: Which one motivates you more?* The Happiness Doctor. https://www.thehappinessdoctor.com/blog/self-compassion-or-self-criticism-motivation

Gordon, E. M., Chauvin, R. J., Van, A. N., Rajesh, A., Nielsen, A., Newbold, D. J., Lynch, C. J., Seider, N. A., Krimmel, S. R., Scheidter, K. M., Monk, J., Miller, R. L., Metoki, A., Montez, D. F., Zheng, A., Elbau, I., Madison, T., Nishino, T., Myers, M. J., & Kaplan, S. (2023). A somato-cognitive action network alternates with effector regions in motor cortex. *Nature, 617,* 1–9. https://doi.org/10.1038/s41586-023-05964-2

Gould, W. R. (2024, March 7). *How to let go of the past and embrace your future.* Verywell Mind. https://www.verywellmind.com/how-to-let-go-of-the-past-8600268

Grande, D. (2024, June 26). *How to stop overthinking.* Psychology Today. https://www.psychologytoday.com/us/blog/in-it-together/202406/stop-overthinking

Greenfield, K. (2020, January 4). *The 4-7-8 breath technique and relaxation exercise.* The Joy Within. https://thejoywithin.org/breath-exercises/4-7-8-breath-technique-and-relaxation-exercise

Grover, S. (2018, July 11). *Where do you store stress in your body? Top 10 secret areas.* Psychology Today. https://www.psychologytoday.com/us/blog/when-kids-call-the-shots/201807/where-do-you-store-stress-in-your-body-top-10-secret-areas

Gupta, A. (2022, April 29). *Are you stuck in the vicious cycle of overthinking? It's risky, warns an expert.* Healthshots. https://www.healthshots.com/mind/mental-health/heres-how-overthinking-can-impact-your-overall-health/

Gupta, S. (2024, April 29). *Feeling anxious? Try the 5-4-3-2-1 grounding technique.* Verywell Mind. https://www.verywellmind.com/5-4-3-2-1-grounding-technique-8639390

Gura, S. (n.d.). *Stop struggling in your life and relationships.* Shira Gura. https://shiragura.com/

Hanh, T. N. (n.d.). *Thich Nhat Hanh quotes*. BrainyQuote. https://www.brainyquote.com/quotes/thich_nhat_hanh_591335

Harvard DCE Professional & Executive Development. (2024, January 9). *How to improve your emotional intelligence*. Professional & Executive Development | Harvard DCE. https://professional.dce.harvard.edu/blog/how-to-improve-your-emotional-intelligence/

Heartwell, S. (2019, April 22). *The art of conscious breathing: A powerful exercise to purify and rejuvenate the body and mind*. Conscious Lifestyle Magazine. https://www.consciouslifestylemag.com/breathing-heal-exercises-body-mind/

Hendriksen, E. (2018, October 29). *The 5 biggest myths of mindfulness*. Scientific American. https://www.scientificamerican.com/article/the-5-biggest-myths-of-mindfulness/

Hoge, E. A., Bui, E., Mete, M., Dutton, M. A., Baker, A. W., & Simon, N. M. (2022). Mindfulness-based stress reduction vs escitalopram for the treatment of adults with anxiety disorders: A randomized clinical trial. *JAMA Psychiatry*, *80*(1), 13–21. https://doi.org/10.1001/jamapsychiatry.2022.3679

Hoshaw, C. (2021, February 9). *How to calm your nervous system*. Healthline. https://www.healthline.com/health/mind-body/give-your-nervous-system-a-break

Hurlburt, R. T., Alderson-Day, B., Kühn, S., & Fernyhough, C. (2016). Exploring the ecological validity of thinking on demand: Neural correlates of elicited vs. spontaneously occurring inner speech. *PLOS ONE*, *11*(2), e0147932. https://doi.org/10.1371/journal.pone.0147932

Hutchison, C. (2023, September 4). *How to journal | the ultimate guide*. Your Visual Journal. https://yourvisualjournal.com/how-to-journal-the-ultimate-guide/

Inagaki, T. K., Bryne Haltom, K. E., Suzuki, S., Jevtic, I., Hornstein, E., Bower, J. E., & Eisenberger, N. I. (2016). The neurobiology of giving versus receiving support. *Psychosomatic Medicine*, *78*(4), 443–453. https://doi.org/10.1097/psy.0000000000000302

Indeed Editorial Team. (2024, July 2). *15 ways to improve your decision-making skills*. Indeed Career Guide. https://www.indeed.com/career-advice/career-development/how-to-improve-decision-making

Jaffe, A. (2024, December 9). *7 strategies for breaking habits that trigger relapse*. Psychology Today. https://www.psychologytoday.com/us/blog/all-about-addiction/202412/7-strategies-for-breaking-habits-that-trigger-relapse

Johanson, D. (2022, February 11). *The science of sadness*. Cosmos. https://cosmosmagazine.com/health/body-and-mind/the-science-of-sadness/

Jones, H. (2023, October 2). *10 exercises that help you stop overthinking.* Verywell Health. https://www.verywellhealth.com/how-to-stop-overthinking-7570368

Kabat-Zinn, J. (2023, December 5). *Wherever you go, there you are: Mindfulness meditation in everyday life; 11th edition.* Hachette Go. https://a.co/d/bAEQMBe

Kaiser, B. N., Haroz, E. E., Kohrt, B. A., Bolton, P. A., Bass, J. K., & Hinton, D. E. (2015). "Thinking too much": A systematic review of a common idiom of distress. *Social Science & Medicine, 147,* 170–183. https://doi.org/10.1016/j.socscimed.2015.10.044

Kane, R. (2024, February 19). *Jon Kabat-Zinn's 9 attitudes of mindfulness (+ PDF).* Mindfulness Box. https://mindfulnessbox.com/the-9-attitudes-of-mindfulness/

Killian, K. (2023, April 25). *How inner monologues work, and who has them.* Psychology Today. https://www.psychologytoday.com/us/blog/intersections/202304/inner-monologues-what-are-they-and-whos-having-them

Koehler, J. (2024, September 18). *Achieving an equilibrium of the mind.* Psychology Today. https://www.psychologytoday.com/sg/blog/beyond-school-walls/202306/achieving-an-equilibrium-of-the-mind

Kuyken, W., Hayes, R., Barrett, B., Byng, R., Dalgleish, T., Kessler, D., Lewis, G., Watkins, E., Brejcha, C.,

Cardy, J., Causley, A., Cowderoy, S., Evans, A., Gradinger, F., Kaur, S., Lanham, P., Morant, N., Richards, J., Shah, P., & Sutton, H. (2015). Effectiveness and cost-effectiveness of mindfulness-based cognitive therapy compared with maintenance antidepressant treatment in the prevention of depressive relapse or recurrence (PREVENT): a randomised controlled trial. *The Lancet, 386*(9988), 63–73. https://doi.org/10.1016/s0140-6736(14)62222-4

Langshur, E., & Klemp, N. (2021, November 1). *How to make gratitude a daily habit.* Mindful. https://www.mindful.org/how-to-make-gratitude-a-daily-habit/

Leahy, R. (2021, April 11). *How to overcome perfectionism.* Psychology Today. https://www.psychologytoday.com/us/blog/anxiety-files/202104/how-to-overcome-perfectionism

Levine, G. N., Cohen, B. E., Commodore-Mensah, Y., Fleury, J., Huffman, J. C., Khalid, U., Labarthe, D. R., Lavretsky, H., Michos, E. D., Spatz, E. S., & Kubzansky, L. D. (2021). Psychological health, well-being, and the mind-heart-body connection: A scientific statement from the american heart association. *Circulation, 143*(10). https://doi.org/10.1161/cir.0000000000000947

Lewandowski, G. (2023, March 7). *How worrying and overthinking can ruin your relationship.* Psychology Today. https://www.psychologytoday.com/us/blog/the-

psychology-of-relationships/202303/how-worrying-
and-overthinking-can-ruin-your

Lim, A. (2022, April 4). *Using Your Body to Express More Than Emotion*. Traditional Chinese Medicine World Foundation. https://www.tcmworld.org/using-your-body-express-more-than-emotion/

Lim, A. (2023, January 26). *The role of emotions in health and healing*. Traditional Chinese Medicine World Foundation. https://www.tcmworld.org/role-emotions-health-healing/

Lindberg, S. (2023, March 21). *How to let go of things from the past*. Healthline. https://www.healthline.com/health/how-to-let-go

Lonczak, H. S. (2020, November 17). *36 ways to find a silver lining during challenging times*. Positive Psychology. https://positivepsychology.com/find-a-silver-lining/#techniques

Lyon, R. A. (2024, October 17). *15 strategies to stop overthinking and find peace of mind*. Senior Fitness. https://www.seniorfitness.org/how-to-stop-overthinking/

Mara. (2024, April 14). *How to effectively stop overthinking and enjoy life*. Important Enough. https://importantenough.com/how_to_stop_overthinking/

Marie, S. (2022, April 15). *10 mental health benefits of pets*. Psych Central. https://psychcentral.com/health/pets-and-mental-health

Martins, I. L. (2020, July 6). *How to practice positive self-talk*. Ivan Leal Martins.

https://www.ivanlealmartins.com/blog/how-to-practice-positive-self-talk

Marut, J. (2016, September 28). *4 ways to remain centered amid all of life's chaos*. Tiny Buddha. https://tinybuddha.com/blog/4-ways-to-remain-centered-amid-all-of-the-chaos/

McAdam, E. (2021, July 9). *Skill #20 intrusive thoughts and overthinking: The skill of cognitive defusion - therapy in a nutshell*. Therapy in a Nutshell. https://therapyinanutshell.com/skill-20-intrusive-thoughts-and-overthinking-the-skill-of-cognitive-defusion/

McCallum, K. (2021, April 12). *When overthinking becomes a problem & what you can do about it*. Houston Methodist. https://www.houstonmethodist.org/blog/articles/2021/apr/when-overthinking-becomes-a-problem-and-what-you-can-do-about-it/

McQuillan, S. (2024, June 28). *What is your inner voice telling you?* Psychology Today. https://www.psychologytoday.com/us/blog/cravings/202406/what-is-your-inner-voice-telling-you

Merriam-Webster. (n.d.-a). *Neuroplasticity*. In Merriam-Webster.com Dictionary. Retrieved October 5, 2024, from https://www.merriam-webster.com/dictionary/neuroplasticity

Merriam-Webster. (n.d.-b). *Plastic*. In Merriam-Webster.com Dictionary. Retrieved October 5, 2024, from https://www.merriam-webster.com/dictionary/plastic

Meyer, L. (2021, September 24). *5 mindful steps for self-observation*. Psychology Today. https://www.psychologytoday.com/intl/blog/mindful-recovery/202109/5-mindful-steps-self-observation

Milbrand, L. (2023, June 29). *The 3-2-8 TikTok workout you might want to try*. Real Simple. https://www.realsimple.com/the-3-2-8-tiktok-workout-you-might-want-to-try-7555470

Miller, K. (2020, March 13). *Building self-awareness: 16 activities and tools for meaningful change*. Positive Psychology. https://positivepsychology.com/building-self-awareness-activities/

Mind-body linkage is built into the structure of the brain, study reveals. (2023, April 17). News-Medical.net. https://www.news-medical.net/news/20230419/Mind-body-

linkage-is-built-into-the-structure-of-the-brain-study-reveals.aspx

Mindful Staff. (2024, December 16). *How to practice gratitude*. Mindful. https://www.mindful.org/an-introduction-to-mindful-gratitude/

Mindfulness meditation: A research-proven way to reduce stress. (2019, October 30). American Psychological Association.

https://www.apa.org/topics/mindfulness/meditatio
n

Moe, K. (2021, June 4). *5 visualization techniques to help you reach your goals.* Betterup. https://www.betterup.com/blog/visualization

Moore, C. (2024, November 7). *What is flow in psychology? Definition and 10+ activities to induce flow.* Positive Psychology. https://positivepsychology.com/what-is-flow/

Morin, A. (2023, November 3). *Healthy coping skills for uncomfortable emotions.* Verywell Mind. https://www.verywellmind.com/forty-healthy-coping-skills-4586742

Morin, A. (2024a, February 21). *9 little habits that make you a better decision maker.* Verywell Mind. https://www.verywellmind.com/habits-for-better-decision-making-4153045

Morin, A. (2024b, June 16). *How to stop overthinking.* Verywell Mind. https://www.verywellmind.com/how-to-know-when-youre-overthinking-5077069

Most women think too much, overthinkers often drink too much. (2003, February 4). University of Michigan News. https://news.umich.edu/most-women-think-too-much-overthinkers-often-drink-too-much/

Myler, C. (2024, June 4). *Stop overthinking now: 18 ways to control your mind again.* Science of People. https://www.scienceofpeople.com/stop-overthinking/

Nicks, S. (1977). *Dreams [Song]. On Rumours.* Warner Records.
https://genius.com/Fleetwood-mac-dreams-lyrics

Nolen-Hoeksema, S. (2004). *Women who think too much.* Henry
Holt and Company.

Online Etymology Dictionary. (n.d.). *Neuro.* In Online
Etymology Dictionary. Retrieved October 5, 2024,
from
https://www.etymonline.com/search?q=neuro

Oppland, M. (2016, December 16). *8 ways to create flow
according to Mihaly
Csikszentmihalyi.* Positive Psychology.
https://positivepsychology.com/mihaly-
csikszentmihalyi-father-of-flow/

Parker, M. (2023, May 20). *Stop overthinking: A practical guide to
finding peace of mind and letting go.* OCBF Press.
https://a.co/d/7ShS7iy

Parvez, H. (2024, July 13). *Cognitive behavioural theory explained.*
PsychMechanics.
https://www.psychmechanics.com/cognitive-
behavioural-theory-cbt-in/

Passaler, L. (2023, May 12). *Nervous system regulation: How to
start regulating your nervous system.* Heal Your Nervous
System.
https://healyournervoussystem.com/nervous-
system-regulation-how-to-start-regulating-your-
nervous-system/

Pattemore, C. (2022, May 27). *How to get started with practicing mindfulness.* Psych Central. https://psychcentral.com/health/new-to-mindfulness-how-to-get-started

Pawula, S. (2021, June 13). *A simple way to balance your emotions and revitalize your body.* Always Well Within. https://always-well-within.squarespace.com/blog/2013/02/17/balance-your-emotions-and-body

Pedersen, T. (2022, May 6). *7 tips for improving your self-awareness.* Psych Central. https://psychcentral.com/health/how-to-be-more-self-aware-and-why-its-important

Pelini, S. (2024, June 25). *An age-by-age guide to helping kids manage emotions.* The Gottman Institute. https://www.gottman.com/blog/age-age-guide-helping-kids-manage-emotions/

Positive Affirmations. (2023, October 4). *The art of mindfulness: How to stay calm and centered in a chaotic world.* Medium. https://medium.com/@positiveaffirmations91/the-art-of-mindfulness-how-to-stay-calm-and-centered-in-a-chaotic-world-7111ec455497

Ranganathan, V. K., Siemionow, V., Liu, J. Z., Sahgal, V., & Yue, G. H. (2004). From mental power to muscle power--gaining strength by using the mind. *Neuropsychologia, 42*(7), 944–956. https://doi.org/10.1016/j.neuropsychologia.2003.1 1.018

Ray, A. (n.d.). *Amit Ray quotes*. Goodreads. https://www.goodreads.com/quotes/10112922-overthinking-is-not-a-disease-it-is-due-to-the

Raypole, C. (2020, April 22). *7 emotion-focused coping techniques for uncertain times*.

Healthline. https://www.healthline.com/health/emotion-focused-coping

Razdan, B. L. (2023, August 20). *Training the brain to be happy*. Greater Kashmir. https://www.greaterkashmir.com/opinion/training-the-brain-to-be-happy/

Rebecca. (2023, July 19). *12 practical tips to help you deal with an overthinker*. Minimalism Made Simple. https://www.minimalismmadesimple.com/home/how-to-deal-with-an-overthinker/

Reed, P. (2021, December 15). *Physical activity is good for the mind and the body*. U.S. Department of Health and Human Services. https://health.gov/news/202112/physical-activity-good-mind-and-body

Regan, S. (2021, January 18). *How to listen to your own inner voice & why it's so important*. Mindbodygreen. https://www.mindbodygreen.com/articles/listen-to-your-inner-voice

Rice, A. (2021, October 26). *Yoga for anxiety: 9 poses to try*. Psych Central. https://psychcentral.com/anxiety/yoga-for-anxiety

Ridley, Y. (2024, February 5). *How to grounded yourself: 6 grounding techniques*. Put the Kettle On. https://putthekettleon.ca/how-to-stay-grounded-and-centered-in-life/

Roest, A. M., Martens, E. J., de Jonge, P., & Denollet, J. (2010). Anxiety and risk of incident coronary heart disease. *Journal of the American College of Cardiology*, *56*(1), 38–46. https://doi.org/10.1016/j.jacc.2010.03.034

Russell, M. (2021, September 24). *How to slow down: 20 simple ways to slow down & enjoy life*. Simple Lionheart Life. https://simplelionheartlife.com/how-to-slow-down/

Sabater, V. (2023, June 7). *Naikan therapy: The healing art of self-reflection*. Exploring Your Mind. https://exploringyourmind.com/naikan-therapy-the-healing-art-of-self-reflection/

Sabater, V. (2024, April 8). *Seven Differences Between Mental and Emotional Health*. Exploring Your Mind. https://exploringyourmind.com/differences-between-mental-and-emotional-health/

Sander, V. (2022, November 9). *How to stop overthinking social interaction (for introverts)*. SocialSelf. https://socialself.com/blog/stop-overthinking/

Santos-Longhurst, A. (2024, January 25). *What are the symptoms and causes of high cortisol levels?* Healthline. https://www.healthline.com/health/high-cortisol-symptoms#what-it-is

Schacht, E. (2021). Wellness tips nurturing a positive mindset. In *University of Iowa.*

https://medicine.uiowa.edu/md/sites/medicine.uiowa.edu.md/files/wysiwyg_uploads/Wellness%20Tips%20Mindset_052721.pdf

Schaffner, A. K. (2023, June 8). *Equanimity: The holy grail of calmness & grace?* Positive Psychology. https://positivepsychology.com/equanimity/

Schembra, C. (2024, September 5). *Intelligent selfishness: How giving to others enriches your own life.* Rolling Stone. https://www.rollingstone.com/culture-council/articles/intelligent-selfishness-giving-others-enriches-own-life-1235094815/

Schultz, J. (2020, July 24). *5 differences between mindfulness and meditation.* Positive Psychology. https://positivepsychology.com/differences-between-mindfulness-meditation/

Scott, E. (2023, October 23). *How to set and crush your goals with way less stress.* Verywell Mind. https://www.verywellmind.com/goal-setting-and-reaching-goals-3145004

Scott, E. (2024, April 2). *How to develop a healthier outlook and learn to be perfectly imperfect.* Verywell Mind. https://www.verywellmind.com/overcoming-perfectionism-how-to-work-past-perfectionism-3144700

Seaver, M. (2023, August 9). *What mindfulness does to your brain: The science of neuroplasticity.* Real Simple.

https://www.realsimple.com/health/mind-mood/mindfulness-improves-brain-health-neuroplasticity

Seaver, M. (2024, April 26). *12 everyday habits to train your brain to be happier.* Real Simple. https://www.realsimple.com/how-to-be-happier-7485523

Shapero, B. G., Greenberg, J., Pedrelli, P., de Jong, M., & Desbordes, G. (2018). Mindfulness-Based interventions in psychiatry. *FOCUS*, *16*(1), 32–39. https://doi.org/10.1176/appi.focus.20170039

Sowers, K. M., Rowe, W. S., & Clay, J. R. (2009). The intersection between physical health and mental health: A global perspective. *Journal of Evidence-Based Social Work*, *6*(1), 111–126. https://doi.org/10.1080/15433710802633734

Sperber, S. (n.d.). *Overthinking: Definition, causes, & how to stop.* The Berkeley Well-Being Institute. https://www.berkeleywellbeing.com/overthinking.html

Stanborough, R. J. (2023, June 5). *How to change negative thinking with cognitive restructuring.* Healthline. https://www.healthline.com/health/cognitive-restructuring

Steffen, P. R., Austin, T., & DeBarros, A. (2016). Treating chronic stress to address the growing problem of depression and anxiety. *Policy Insights from the*

Behavioral and Brain Sciences, *4*(1), 64–70. https://doi.org/10.1177/2372732216685333

Stone, J. (2024, October 22). *Men and the hidden costs of overthinking.* Psychology Today. https://www.psychologytoday.com/us/blog/the-souls-of-men/202409/men-and-the-hidden-costs-of-overthinking

Stress. (n.d.). Mind. https://www.mind.org.uk/information-support/types-of-mental-health-problems/stress/causes-of-stress/

Stress. (2024, May 20). Cleveland Clinic. https://my.clevelandclinic.org/health/diseases/11874-stress

Strick, M., Dijksterhuis, A., & van Baaren, R. B. (2010). Unconscious-thought effects take place off-line, not on-line. *Psychological Science*, *21*(4), 484–488. https://doi.org/10.1177/0956797610363555

Sutton, J. (2021, November 19). How to overcome perfectionism: 15 worksheets & resources. *Positive Psychology.* https://positivepsychology.com/how-to-overcome-perfectionism/

The Editorial Team. (2022, November 29). *Daniel Goleman's emotional intelligence theory explained.* Resilient Educator. https://resilienteducator.com/classroom-resources/daniel-golemans-emotional-intelligence-theory-explained/

The overthinking epidemic: Is modern society encouraging us to think too much? (2023, June 30). A Life Well Lived.

https://www.alife-welllived.com/blog/theoverthinkingepidemic

Therapy in a Nutshell. (2021). Intrusive thoughts and overthinking: The skill of cognitive defusion 20/30 [video]. In *YouTube*. https://www.youtube.com/watch?v=V3vhXQy48jo

Therapy in a Nutshell. (2022). Catastrophizing: How to stop making yourself depressed and anxious: Cognitive distortion skill #6 [Video]. In *YouTube*. https://www.youtube.com/watch?v=bS2LPNlO07s

Therapy in a Nutshell. (2023a). Automatic negative thoughts - break the anxiety cycle 11/30 [Video]. In *YouTube*. https://www.youtube.com/watch?v=lLZ-3TSoe9E

Therapy in a Nutshell. (2023b, November 9). *How to stop overthinking: Master the*

ACT skill of cognitive defusion 13/30. YouTube. https://www.youtube.com/watch?v=OhNm7ZSiZls

Therapy in a Nutshell. (2024, January 4). *Emotional reasoning-the cognitive distortion that makes you emotionally reactive - anxiety 18/30 [Video].* YouTube. https://www.youtube.com/watch?v=YBzvkgARehg

Tokeikyte, G. (2021, March 22). *Why we fall back into old habits when we're tired or stressed.* Psychology Today. https://www.psychologytoday.com/us/blog/yes-you-can/202103/why-we-fall-back-into-old-habits-when-were-tired-or-stressed

Tsaousides, T. (2023, July 23). *How many emotions can you feel?* Psychology Today. https://www.psychologytoday.com/us/blog/smashing-the-brainblocks/202307/how-many-emotions-are-there

Tsatiris, D. (2021, September 10). *Three practical tips to overcome perfectionism.* Psychology Today. https://www.psychologytoday.com/us/blog/anxiety-in-high-achievers/202109/three-practical-tips-to-overcome-perfectionism

U.S. Department of Health and Human Services. (2018). Physical activity guidelines for Americans 2nd edition. In *U.S. Department of Health and Human Services* (pp. 8–10). https://health.gov/sites/default/files/2019-09/Physical_Activity_Guidelines_2nd_edition.pdf

Vandervort, S. (2024, May 29). *Get out of your head and into your body with these five practices.* The Local Mystic. https://thelocalmystic.com/get-out-of-your-head-five-practices/

Viezzer, S. (2024, February 5). *How to improve emotional intelligence.* Simply Psychology. https://www.simplypsychology.org/how-to-improve-emotional-intelligence.html

Washington University School of Medicine. (2023, April 20). *Hidden linkages: Scientists find mind-body connection is built into brain.* SciTechDaily. https://scitechdaily.com/hidden-linkages-scientists-find-mind-body-connection-is-built-into-brain/

Wegner, D. (1990, June 1). *White bears and other unwanted thoughts: Suppression, obsession, and the psychology of mental control.* Penguin Books. https://a.co/d/iKczKER

Wegner, D. (2011, November). *Setting free the bears: Escape from thought suppression.* American Psychologist. https://dtg.sites.fas.harvard.edu/DANWEGNER/pub/Setting%20free%20the%20bears%202011.pdf

Wegner, D. M., & Schneider, D. J. (2003). The white bear story. *Psychological Inquiry, 14*(3/4), 326–329. https://www.jstor.org/stable/1449696

Weil, A. (2006, May 8). *Richard Davidson.* TIME. https://content.time.com/time/specials/packages/article/0,28804,1975813_1975844_1976433,00.html

Why laughing is good for you. (2024, August 29). Cleveland Clinic. https://health.clevelandclinic.org/is-laughing-good-for-you

Wignall, N. (2021, November 4). *10 simple ways to improve your self-awareness [with examples].* Nick Wignall. https://nickwignall.com/self-awareness/

Williams, C. (2022, July 4). *How to understand your inner voice and control your inner critic.* New Scientist. https://www.newscientist.com/article/mg25533941-100-how-to-understand-your-inner-voice-and-control-your-inner-critic/

Winzeler, M. (2020, May 27). *Calm your body and mind: A therapist's guide for nervous system regulation.* WellnessWinz. https://wellnesswinz.com/2020/05/27/calm-your-body-and-mind-a-therapists-guide-for-nervous-system-regulation/

Working out boosts brain health. (2020, March 4). American Psychological Association. https://www.apa.org/topics/exercise-fitness/stress

World Health Organization. (2022, March 2). *COVID-19 pandemic triggers 25% increase in prevalence of anxiety and depression worldwide.* World Health Organization. https://www.who.int/news/item/02-03-2022-covid-19-pandemic-triggers-25-increase-in-prevalence-of-anxiety-and-depression-worldwide

Yeshurun, Y., Nguyen, M., & Hasson, U. (2021). The default mode network: Where the idiosyncratic self meets the shared social world. *Nature Reviews Neuroscience, 22.* https://doi.org/10.1038/s41583-020-00420-w

Yun, R. C., Fardghassemi, S., & Joffe, H. (2022). Thinking too much: How young people experience rumination in the context of loneliness. *Journal of Community & Applied Social Psychology.* https://doi.org/10.1002/casp.2635